PAST THE GRAY CURTAIN

My Road to Full Life with Disability

SARAH BLAKE LAROSE

ISBN-13: 979-8-9930506-0-7 (Paperbook)
ISBN-13: 979-8-9930506-1-4 (Ebook)

To purchase this book in braille, please visit us on the web:
www.night-light.org

Cover and interior formatting by:
KUHN Design Group | kuhndesigngroup.com

This book tells the stories of people who have played important roles in my life and who are now at rest from their physical labors. May their memory live on through the stories I tell:

Ferne Schneider Erickson

Elaine Johnson

Shelva Jean Pickler

Vicki Johnston

Dr. Michael Trese

Judi Sorah

ACKNOWLEDGEMENTS

This book is in your hands today because of the support of my mom and my husband. My mom has been the assistant who describes images and colors to me so that I can decide what I want in my book design. She is a visual thinker and knows what is pretty. She also knows colors that are beautiful to me personally. I believe that she has helped me to work with Steve Kuhn to bring you a book that represents my heart.

My husband, Kevin, pored over this manuscript for many hours, picking apart my text and helping me to speak more clearly. He said to me one day, "You talked in this place about your cat, but you haven't said that you had a cat yet." He put a note in the file for me to "move the cat around."

Kevin is gifted with the ability to read thoroughly and give critical feedback. He has helped tell my story without wandering, getting ahead, or repeating.

I promise that the cat is in just the right place—and does not have the zoomies.

CONTENTS

OPENING THOUGHTS

At several times in my life, people have expressed interest in how I have experienced and thought about life as a person who is blind. I have tried here to collect together some stories and writings that will give voice to that experience.

Many people who meet me probably don't realize that I have any sight or that I have experienced very traumatic loss of that sight—not once but many times.

I have grown up living with blindness and am fortunate to have learned many ways to do things early in my life. These things help me to know how to live practically without sight; but they don't make the emotional response to sight loss easy. I never lost my ability to drive, but I grieved what I lost and experienced spiritual difficulties for a time.

Blindness has been the longest part of my life, so I will talk a lot about it. It is not the only part of my life. I have also experienced other adult-onset disabilities that are, in some ways, more difficult to live with than blindness is.

I hope you will find that you have some things in common

with me whether or not you live with disability. I have experienced deep disappointments and have also found places of deep peace in my life. That is something everyone can understand. I hope my stories will help you to laugh, cry, hope, and think deeply.

I grew up striving to fit into a community that was sighted. My participation in the blind community was, and still is, irregular and complicated.

I began my education just as the legislation was passed that gave children with disabilities the right to attend school with nondisabled peers. I graduated high school in the year that the Americans with Disabilities Act was passed. I am hesitant to romanticize these things too much; but my life is bound up with them in ways both positive and negative.

I did not experience a particular desire to prove that I could do anything exceptional. If I wanted to try something, I did. If I didn't want to do it, no amount of cajoling, convincing, or talking to me about how many other blind people were doing it would change my mind.

I grew up without blind mentors. I have often found it difficult to find people who have done the things I am trying to do. I hope that in sharing my experiences, I can be a "mentor in writing" to someone who needs one.

Several names in my stories have been changed in order to protect the privacy and dignity of particular individuals. I have not identified the individuals whose names have been changed in order to give grace to them. If you find your name or recognize yourself in my story, please know that you have made a positive impact in my life.

If my book is encouraging to you or your community group, please encourage someone else to buy a copy. If you need a braille copy, please visit the web site: www.night-light.org

Shalom.

1

LEARNING TO SEE

Were you born that way?" The question comes at me out of the blue, from a person whose name I might never know. If I answer, the person may ask another question or two and then will probably go away without saying goodbye—while I am still speaking. If I am lucky, they will comment about my beautiful dog or tell me that I am an inspiration to them.

When I talk to people about my blindness, I often say that I was born prematurely. Occasionally a person responds by saying, "Oh, you got too much oxygen?"

Things are a little more complicated than this. But I didn't always know that.

In the early 1950s a large number of premature babies were blinded by overexposure to oxygen. After a few years the oxygen requirements for premature infants were changed, and only those babies who truly needed high levels of oxygen received it. Doctors continued to tell parents that premature babies' blindness was caused by "too much oxygen" even into the 1980s. Over 50 potential causes of the condition have been studied.

In the 1970s, doctors noted that smaller and more premature babies were developing the condition. The name of the condition was changed from retrolental fibroplasia, which described the advanced stages of the condition, to retinopathy of prematurity, which associated all stages of the condition with premature birth. New screening techniques became available for babies who were very young, and treatments were developed which could halt the progress of the condition at early stages and prevent blindness for many babies.

I was born at the time when the old terminology was still in use and no treatments were available. My parents talked very openly with me about what they knew about my eye condition. They even taught me to spell it: RETROLENTAL FIBROPLASIA (RLF).

When I was in the fourth grade, kids were bragging about the longest word they could spell. I thought it was really cool that I could spell the entire phrase. The only problem was that someone would probably ask, "What's that?" and I couldn't explain it except to say, "It's my eye condition." If I said this, some smarty-pants—probably a boy—would say, "So, what is it?" If I couldn't explain it, it didn't really matter that I could spell retrolental fibroplasia.

Spelling words was nothing unusual for me. If a word was interesting to me, I wanted to write it. I was a good speller of plenty of other words, even the hard ones.

My old school records indicate that I didn't become interested in braille the first time I was introduced to it. A year later, another teacher introduced it again and I made a rather speedy start. Not only did I master it quickly, but I was a voracious reader. I devoured books and children's magazines.

I loved all kinds of word games. My braille magazines had word puzzles in them. I thought it was wonderful that I could do crossword puzzles just like my mother. My teacher created word-finding puzzles for me to solve just like the rest of my class. My mother and grandmother taught me to play Scrabble when I was seven years old.

When I practiced my spelling words, I wrote them twice. In braille there are special shorthand signs for combinations of letters. I wrote all of my words once with the shorthand signs and once without:

S-d	s-a-i-d
Sh-ou-t	s h o u t
B	b-u-t
C	c-a-n
t-g-r	t-o-g-e-t-h-e-r

I got so good at spelling that I won the class spelling bee in fifth grade. I thought this was pretty cool, and I didn't think anything else about it.

"You're going to the district spelling bee!" my teacher said excitedly.

What? District? I didn't know there was a district spelling bee! I was just having a little fun in class.

I got the point that I needed to work hard. My teacher sent home a big book of words. My mom spent night after night helping me learn every single word in the drill book.

My hard work paid off. I made it all the way to the regional spelling bee.

The big day for regional finally came. The weather was bright and sunny. What a great day to be inside spelling words!

The room was full of kids and parents. We were all given numbers so that we would not be identified personally. My mom and I thought maybe it was a good-luck charm that I was number 1.

I had only spelled a few words when a problem arose. There were so many kids in the competition that the words in the drill book were getting used up. I was given the word "midriff".

Unfair! I thought. That word was not in the book!

I stood at the microphone, panic-stricken. I took a deep breath and started. "M-i-d..." Ok, I was off to a great start, but I was about to make a total fool of myself with this word. Was there something between the d and the r? "Mid-**riff!**" Just what do I do with that other syllable? Ok, here goes nothing: "R-i-f-f..." Was this one of those evil words with silent e on the end? Oh, why couldn't they have given me a word I had practiced! Fine! Here goes nothing! "E?"

I could feel the air go out of the room and suck me out with it. "I'm sorry, that is incorrect."

My mom escorted me out. The waterworks began. "It's not fair!" I wailed! I wondered why I couldn't have just spelled retrolental fibroplasia.

"It's not so bad," Mom soothed. "Number 2 just came out." Her name was Nancy.

Conspiracy. They were on the side of the smarty-pants boys.

Several years later someone asked me whether I had RLF or

retinopathy of prematurity (ROP). I was nearing the end of high school and had never heard that there was a name change for the condition. Several years went by before I could satisfy my new curiosity. I wanted to know much more than the fact that the condition had a new name. I wanted to know why, and what it meant.

In the 1990s I discovered two things: the Internet and book scanners. After I got a scanner, I began collecting information and educating myself. Reading articles was empowering and helped me to sort through my thoughts and feelings.

In the early 1970s, it was the norm for RLF to be discovered when babies were several months old, after the condition had done its damage. At that point the child would have some degree of blindness ranging from nearly normal sight to no sight at all. Many people had additional problems with their eyes as they grew older. This is what happened to me.

My blindness was diagnosed when I was five months old. Doctors gave my parents some hope that I might have some use of my right eye, but they could not provide any information about what I might be able to see. My parents would have to wait until I was old enough to talk and describe what I could see.

I am sure that this was an agonizing thing for my parents to hear. They did not know anyone who was blind, and they were not referred to any helpful resources. At that time, education services were not widely available for very young children who were blind. I am grateful that they used their own creativity to encourage me to exercise all of my senses through natural entertainment, to encourage me to tolerate things I sometimes did not like, and to simply have fun with me. I am also grateful that they persevered in searching for educational resources.

My mother noted shortly before my first birthday that I began staring at lights. My grandmother also noticed that I seemed to be reacting to colors as I got older. My family learned about what I could and could not see by observing my play and reactions to visual stimuli.

Today I am an adult, and it is not possible for anyone to know precisely what I can see. I can answer that yes, I can see an object that is in front of me, but the way that I see and perceive it is very different from the way that someone else sees and perceives it. I may or may not identify the whole object depending on whether it fits within the small space that I can see in front of me and whether I can perceive details accurately.

My color perception is also very distorted. Dark blue may look black to me. Certain colors are familiar and pleasing to me, but I cannot necessarily identify them by name.

Today children who are deaf or blind are eligible for special education services provided through the state from infancy through high school. When I was very young, this education was not mandated. My parents were not referred to any resources to help them in learning how to encourage my development.

My mother eventually found an educational program for children with disabilities affiliated with a university in Oklahoma City, Oklahoma. The Child Study Center was a blessing for my family.

Part of my education involved learning how to use the sight I had to get information about the environment. Many blind people today have quite negative feelings about this type of intervention because it can lead to failure to provide education in other skills such as braille that are also important. Instruction in use of my sight was not competitive with braille instruction, and I have no regrets. Parents must hold a positive attitude about the importance of all the senses and stimulate them along with the sense of sight.

I had no interest in braille during these very early years. I think there were numerous exciting things for me to explore, and braille would have been too much too soon. I have a few vivid memories of some of the games and other activities that my teachers used to help me with developing the skills to match what I heard and saw with what I touched. We tossed bean bags, and I had to retrieve them from where I heard them dropped. They were made of different textured fabrics, and I became used to touching these in my hands. We took walks in new places, where I learned to step into the unknown. But the activity I remember most vividly had to do with shapes on the wall.

I stood spell-bound by the change in the appearance of the wall. The room was dark except for the wall, which was partially lit up.

Three dark shapes appeared side by side: a triangle, a square, and a circle. I did as my teacher asked—I pointed to the circle. But there was only the image of the circle. I was touching the wall. Why was there no circle to touch?

The shape projecting exercise helped me to develop eye-hand coordination and also taught me to search for things visually. I needed this kind of guidance; for my attention was often not drawn naturally to things which weren't directly in front of me. If it was outside my field of view, it did not seem to exist. I needed to learn that I could look around and explore; and I needed to learn to coordinate the information from my eyes with the movements of my hands in a practical way.

That morning, I learned much more than how to identify shapes visually. I learned that an object could be represented as an abstract image. "Where does that circle come from?" I asked.

My teacher took time out to explain how a projector worked, to let me feel the shapes in the projector, and to allow me to project my own shapes on the wall. I remember very little about my sessions with her—I was little more than three years old. But I remember this one like it was yesterday. The real lesson that morning was about how things worked, and it was about the fact that one can see an image that represents an object that is elsewhere. I began to learn to think "outside the box." Such abstract lessons have served me well throughout my life.

Color-matching games were much harder for me. I was still working on them when I was six years old. Another teacher presented me with three lights: red, blue and green. The only reason why I was ever able to name the color red was that the red light blinked and made a noise. I knew that I should not rely on the blinking and buzzing—I was supposed to recognize the color red with my eye. To admit that I could not see red was to fail the game. I could see white, yellow, green, orange, blue, brown, and black. But I could not see red. And colors did not look the same to me when they came from lights as they looked on paper or on clothing. I could not explain why. They just did not.

Many years later, after I had a cornea transplant, I sat in a doctor's office and admitted that I could not tell him the color of his light. He said irritably, "Anyone can identify red!"

I wanted to punch him for judging the entire usefulness of my sight—and the value of his work—based on my ability to name the color red! My mom and I drove home from the office, which was located in another state, a five-hour drive from our home in Indiana. I held back my tears until I reached home.

I knew the idiom that one saw red when one was angry. I saw red that day.

Doctors spoke honestly to my parents about the possibility that I could develop glaucoma or cataracts in my good eye and that these conditions could threaten my remaining sight. Because of these possibilities, my parents wisely advocated for me to learn braille when I became old enough to begin reading instruction. They also permitted the continuation of instruction in print and other visual skills for as long as I was able to benefit. Today, I have such a small area through which light can enter my eye that doctors are surprised I can see at all. Still, I am able to use that tiny amount of sight for some things that are beneficial. I am convinced that the benefit comes not from the sight itself but from the education in how to integrate it with other senses.

Some of my activities with my teacher included my family, who participated and learned how I moved around as a blind child by watching and listening to the instructions she gave me. My grandmother wrote in a letter to extended family:

My husband and I were privileged to accompany Sarah and her teacher, Wanda, to a beautiful playground, a wonderland of adventure with rope ladders, towers connected by a swinging bridge, poles to slide on and Indian teepees.

Upon our arrival Wanda said, "Come Sarah, let's run through the maze" and they entered a maze made of upright railroad ties. We followed more slowly and when we came to a turning point, we didn't know which way to go. Several times we found ourselves up against a blank wall and we tried several paths before we found our way out of the maze that Sarah had run through so easily. We were trusting our own senses; she was trusting, and following closely, her teacher.

Then Wanda led Sarah to a boardwalk, always walking before her, leading the way. She gave instructions, "This is the boardwalk, rather high off the ground. If you get too close to the edge, you'll fall. Take small steps and if you feel your foot touch the edge, move back to the middle of the walk…. Careful, Sarah, you're getting too close to the edge; move back to the right." And they made it safely, all the way, together.

The teacher then led Sarah to a little hill and set a goal before her. "This is the hill with the two posts on top. See if you can climb up to the posts." Following her instructions, a tiny figure trudged to the top of the hill, circled both posts and then began the descent. "I can't! It's too steep—help me!"

"It's okay, Sarah. Why don't you sit down and slide a bit; then when you come to a place that's not so steep, you can stand up and walk again.

All my grandmotherly instincts urged me to help Sarah, to carry her so she might not fall. But her teacher knew she needed to learn to follow directions, to gain self-confidence and to strengthen those little legs.

Next was a downhill trip—not down the smooth grassy slope that looked so easy—but walking over rocks and ruts, with the teacher again walking the path before her. Sarah was learning how to walk over rough ground; she was learning she could safely follow her leader through the hard places.

Sarah played for a time in a long underground tunnel where she shouted to hear her voice echo. Then she followed Wanda into a cave. Always staying close to her teacher, she made her way through narrow dark passages and came at last into a large room. We came out into the sunlight again and Wanda said, "Sarah, I'm going to the fort. You follow me. There is a muddy place you'll have to cross but it's all right; just follow me." But Sarah didn't want to go through the mud. She walked beside it for some distance, hoping to find a dry place to cross. All the while Wanda was calling to her, "It's all right to step in the mud, Sarah. I'm right here. Come to me." But Sarah was afraid to get her feet wet and turned away and started up the hill. Her teacher called again, "You're going the wrong way. Turn around and come to me." Obediently, Sarah turned and followed her voice. When she came again to the muddy area, Wanda spoke,

"That's the place to cross, right there." And Sarah waded through the mud and. entered the fort where she was free to explore. Sarah then reentered the tunnel. But this time there was some water in the tunnel and suddenly she was afraid. "Is there water in here?"

"Yes, but the water is not deep; it's okay, Sarah."

We could hear the doubt in the childish voice as she asked again, "Will I get my shoes wet?" Then she tripped and fell and in panic, she cried out. Instantly, Wanda was on her hands and knees, crawling into the tunnel to bring out the frightened child.

…How did she know Sarah could learn to walk through a world she could not see? Wanda, as a part of her training, had made her way in public places wearing a heavy blindfold. She had eaten in restaurants and played in the park as a blind person. She knew from experience the fears and frustrations that come when you can't see.

I was very blessed to have a teacher who had entered my world at the age of three. She empowered me to move around in the environment with confidence when the only exploration tool I had was my own body.

When I was four years old, my family moved to Houston, Texas. There we had better access to educational resources for me. We also lived near my mom's parents. Both of these things were important as I grew older.

ENCOURAGEMENT FOR PARENTS

I often see notes from parents on social media asking what to do since they don't know how much their child can see. It is very anxiety-provoking to not be able to get a definitive test that shows a numerical measurement indicating how a child sees in comparison to themselves.

My words probably will not put those anxieties to much rest, but I will say them anyway.

Play with your child. Having a test result will not change who your child is. Your child is there, waiting for you to discover their personality and enjoyment. It is ok to play with light-up toys, and if you find your child doesn't respond to them, give them up. Be sure that you also play with noisy toys, fuzzy toys, toys with all kinds of textures, and be responsive to that good-smelling food that's cooking in the kitchen. All these things will help your child to become a curious learner and engage with the environment.

Move around—a lot—and encourage your child to move. It won't hurt them to get bumps and bruises. Your sighted child will get bumps and bruises falling off their bikes. Don't shield your blind child from this. Moving around is how they orient themselves.

Most of all, allow blindness to become a factoid, like your height. If you are sad about it, give yourself a crying period and then move to the next thing. Your child will not be sad most of the time. Sadness about blindness is provoked by society's attitudes, not by the experience of blindness itself.

2

I AM DIFFERENT

Today it is common for young blind children to have their days filled with school and therapy sessions. I am glad that children and families have more resources available. On the other hand, I am also glad that I was able to simply grow in relationships with my family and community without my days being strictly governed by educational and therapeutic schedules.

My earliest memories are about having fun and feeling loved. I grew up with a great curiosity about the world around me that I am confident came from being in the world that my family and community participated in. My mom often said, "We've got places to go and people to see." Wherever we went, I was curious and ready.

MUSIC, PLAY, AND THE CHURCH

For as long as I can remember, my mom has played the piano for whatever church she attended. I heard the sound of the piano at home as she practiced. I was drawn to it, and I wanted to know how she made that sound. I enjoyed the music and loved to put my hands on the keyboard while she played. She was gracious and allowed this as long as I did not press the keys. I learned that she made the pretty music by making some of the keys go down while others stayed up.

I also enjoyed imitating my family members' voices. My family loved to make funny sounds, and I mimicked them to the best of my ability. Mom decided one day to see if I understood high and low notes. "Sing a high note," she said. I sang a high note with gusto. Then I asked her to do a low note.

She sang an ugly, guttural low note, and I mimicked her in tone. My voice could not reach her low pitch.

My early childhood teacher noted that I "played with abandon." Early recordings that my mother has given to me seem to reflect this. I ran around the room, climbing into the laps of anyone and everyone, demanding attention until it was given. I sang freely, not caring who heard or what they thought of my made-up lyrics. I turned pages in a Bible and my grandmother asked, "What does the Bible say?" I proclaimed, "God loves my God!" My grandmother repeated my words as if I had just prophesied the best heavenly word.

I was so care-free that my family was concerned that I would get into an unsafe situation without knowing, or that other people would not realize what I could not see. At church, I learned the layout of the building and felt confident in my ability to wander around. Had anyone asked, I could have guided them to any classroom, any of the offices, the nurseries, or the sanctuary. However, my parents and grandparents kept hold of my hand when the church was full of people. My frustration with this situation is evident in my grandmother's one-line memory: "Holding her own hand as she ran down the hall."

When the church was emptied of people, it was a fascinating place to explore. There were hard floors to clomp on, carpets to be very quiet on, and hallways to talk in and listen for echoes…

My grandfather was responsible for locking all the buildings. One day, he took me with him on his door-locking rounds. We went into the building where the Sunday school classrooms were located, and I laughed as my voice echoed down the empty hallway.

"You say something," I said, thinking it would be fun to hear his booming voice echo.

"I can imitate a donkey," he said.

"You can't sound like a donkey!" I laughed.

Gramps took a great big breath and let out an awful braying sound: "Heehawwwww! Hee-hawwwwww! Hee-hawwwww!!!!!" The donkey sound echoed down the hallway.

"Do it again!" I said as he turned off the lights. The great sound came again. I wondered if my mother could hear it in the main church building and if Gramps and I would get in trouble for playing in the classroom building. Then again, who could punish Gramps! He was the one with the keys!

PLAYMATES AND BOOKS

I had a playmate from church, Debbie. Debbie and I loved to play with books. I remember taking them down from her father's bookshelves and sitting side by side flipping pages. I was often attracted to the dark blobs which I knew were pictures. Of course, I didn't know what they were. It didn't matter. Neither I nor Debbie could read, so we made up our own content; and since we were flipping through big, fat grown-up books it didn't matter what we were "reading". But when we started school, Debbie became able to point out things like the fact that there were no words on that page. Our "reading" wasn't just play anymore. Debbie was beginning to read; I was pretending.

Soon Debbie and I "grew apart". I'm sure there were a number of reasons for this, but I only knew that she didn't talk to me at church anymore, and she didn't want to play with me when her family came to our house. I could not verbalize my feelings, but I remember wondering if it was because I couldn't read.

I thought that going to kindergarten might give me something fun to talk about with Debbie. We were doing the same thing, after all. I soon learned that my kindergarten wasn't like hers. First, there were only six kids in my class. I thought kindergarten had a lot of kids.

Next, all the other kids were much older than I was. I was the only one who was five years old. All the other kids at church who were in kindergarten were five. In my class most of the others were six, and one was seven! Kids really do notice this stuff!

In my kindergarten class, we had a number line on the floor. Big black numbers were drawn on squares and placed in front of a row of chairs where we sat. Every day, we all walked the number line and counted from one to ten before putting our belongings in our cubbies. I could see the numbers, and I thought everything was normal.

Then I got a braille writer: a big metal machine with six keys for my fingers and a special "space bar" in the middle. I learned how to roll paper into it like a typewriter. When I pressed the keys, dots came up on the paper!

I also got my own braille books! They were enticing things with drawings made with string and felt and cotton, and braille labels. And no printed pictures.

My books were different from anyone else's books. My parents' books didn't have braille, and neither did any of my friends' books, or their parents' books, or my grandparents' books. It should have made me feel special.

This forever changed the way that I played with friends. No one was interested in my books, and I couldn't play with theirs. We were left with Barbies. But by that time kids were not playing barbies much. They were outside, riding skateboards and bikes.

My books became my friends. I needed lots of books. All the time. I read all of my braille books very quickly and wanted more. So, I was introduced to cassettes and records as ways to read. I learned to gently put cassettes into a special machine that played them very slowly and split the cassettes into four sides instead of two. I learned how to very gently put a needle onto a vinyl record so that it would start at just the right time and would not scratch. I had hours and hours of fun reading— in any way I wanted.

Reading was fun, and I always enjoyed it. But I so loved to

be outside…And I wanted to play with friends! My personal theme lyric could have been, "Don't wanna be all by myself!"[1]

FIRST NEIGHBORHOOD FRIEND

Shortly before my fifth birthday, I met my first neighborhood friend. I was not expecting to meet anyone. I was just spending time outside with my dad. He had just mowed the grass. I loved the smell of freshly cut grass! I also loved to dive into his piles of leaves and make them rustle and crunch.

"There's a little girl next door," Dad said casually.

A little girl? Perhaps she might play with me, I thought.

I walked away from where Dad was raking leaves and stopped at the tree which served as a marker for the imaginary boundary between my yard and the neighbors' yard. Peering shyly around the tree, I saw her: a little girl about my size wearing pink.

I remember the meeting today as if it happened yesterday. I was almost five years old; Jill was six. Her grandparents were the owners of the house next door. From that day on, we played together whenever she visited them. Sometimes our play lasted only long enough for us to drink a glass of Coke. Sometimes she spent the night, and we made tents with blankets over couches and chairs in the living room and played Little House on the Prairie.

Jill and I did not always live in the same neighborhood, but the friendship we forged was strong. We didn't need to be in the neighborhood in order to continue doing friend things.

---

1. "All By Myself" lyrics © Eric Carmen Music, Round Hill Works, Hawkes & Son (London) Ltd., Boosey & Hawkes Music Publishers Ltd.

Several years after we met, her family went deer hunting and invited me to go along to their cabin. It was turning cold, and we decorated Styrofoam balls to hang on the Christmas tree. I remember walking down the road together, and suddenly Jill told me to stop. "We're coming to a cattle guard." She described it to me and told me that I would need to step carefully on the rails so that my toes did not get caught. I was terrified that suddenly a bunch of cattle might come stampeding through and trample us, but I trusted Jill to know what to do. This was her place.

Being at Jill's family's cabin was probably as educational for me as any of the community activities I participated in later with groups of blind children. It was special because it was something I did with Jill, and there were no adults intervening to show me what to do. It was Jill who taught me to walk on the cattle guard, and that is something I will probably remember for the rest of my life.

SEEKING MORE FRIENDS

When my family moved to a new neighborhood, I thought that if I was outside playing, I might meet a new friend in the same way that I met Jill. I had shown up. I wouldn't be able to see them, and Dad wasn't raking leaves just then. But I knew they were outside playing—I could hear them screaming and laughing. So, I took some toys outside and settled down to play—and, hopefully, to be seen.

I could not see what other children were doing across the street. In fact, if I heard them playing and my ears told me they were across the street, the reality might be that they were in the back yard of the house across the street.

If my parents had understood that a blind child could travel independently and safely, they might have oriented me to the neighborhood so that I could venture out and meet children in other yards. My blindness did not allow me to recognize our house or other people's faces, and at that point in my life none of us had ever seen a cane. Circumstance forced me to wait passively for other children to show interest in me.

Other children did not show interest. Day after day, I went outside to play—to prove to those other children that I knew how to have fun too. I roller-skated up and down the sidewalk in front of my house. I had picnics with my dolls. I bounced a ball. I turned somersaults in the yard...None of these things enticed any of the neighborhood children to come and play. Why? Didn't they want another playmate? Didn't they think I might like to play? I thought about Jill and wondered why other children didn't feel about me the way I had felt about her.

That couldn't be it. Surely, they enjoyed playing with other children. I could hear them playing together. But I concluded that I was not wanted as a playmate. Something must be wrong with me. Why else wouldn't they want me? What was wrong with me? What was so different about me?

I was sure that I knew the answer. I was blind. And I wasn't allowed to go out of my parents' sight. How I would love to go roller skating down the block or ride a bike around the neighborhood! But I had to stop at the third house, turn around, and come back. I was certain that the sidewalk past the third house must be just like the rest of the sidewalk. In fact, I had walked on it a few times with my babysitter and my dad. But I dutifully turned around and went back home, always wishing for more places to roller skate.

At that time in my life, I did not understand that the children might have been too immersed in their own play to know or care who was across the street or down the block. I did not understand that something could have obstructed their view and thus kept them from seeing me. One can hear things she cannot necessarily see; but in my mind I was aware of them, so they must be aware of me.

Neither did I understand that my inability to reach out was most likely a bigger handicap than my blindness. I only understood that I was alone, and they were not. The knowledge of my aloneness made me think and wonder…I came to the conclusion that blindness was the reason for my aloneness. I perceived myself as rejected—and I began to act like someone who had been rejected. All the love and support my parents gave me could not give me playmates; and as I began to perceive through my observations of my peers' interactions and the plots of stories I read that the norm was to have playmates, my desire and the accompanying perception that I was flawed intensified.

3

TSB

During the summer after my seventh birthday, I was enrolled in a six-week program at the Texas School for the Blind (TSB). The program was a six-week program. The first person I met was my roommate, Penny. We talked for a few minutes, and then she went next door to visit another girl, Cathy. They kept using words like "half blind" and "partially blind" as if they were badges of honor. It made me feel all squirmy, as if I was supposed to compare my sight to theirs.

I wandered across the hall to meet the girls who lived there. Becky had opened the closet door so that it covered a portion of the doorway to the hall. "When it's like this," she said curtly, "don't come in."

Lindsay was in the next room. She came out of her room and let me lead her across the hall. She sat beside me on my bed, still holding my hand but fidgeting nervously. She was nine years old. Every so often, she would start to cry. She couldn't tell me why.

LOST

My mother offered to take me and Lindsay to the playground. I thought this would be a good idea. Maybe Lindsay was homesick and lonely. I wanted to be her friend.

Lindsay tagged along, still holding my hand, still crying. I don't remember what we did on the playground, but I know that we were not there for a very long time. Lindsay didn't seem to feel like playing. My parents took us back inside and dropped her off at her room.

Penny and Cathy were very friendly. They were a year older than I and seemed to know their way around. They also had more vision; and Penny wasn't bothered by other children's taunts about her lack of glasses. "I don't have to wear glasses," she said matter-of-factly. "I'm only half blind," she said when someone asked if we were totally blind.

Was I totally blind? Or was I "half blind?" I didn't answer. I didn't know what "half blind" meant. Did it mean you could read the big E on the eye chart? How far away did you have to be when you read the big E to be considered "half blind?" My parents never used these terms when they talked to people about me. They told people that I had "light perception" or that I was just "blind".

I could see shades of color, buildings and driveways as we drove past in the car. Wasn't that more than "light perception"? But it probably wasn't "half blind".

I figured out that Penny and Cathy could see a lot better than I could. They could recognize each other in a small group, probably by picking out each other's hair and clothing. They probably didn't have to walk all the way up to the wall to read the big E. And for some reason, this mattered. Where did I belong? Was there such a thing as "three fourths blind"?

I was happy to deliver Lindsay back to her room, where she seemed peaceful. But I wasn't done trying to play. Since Penny and Cathy seemed familiar with the grounds, I decided to go out and play with them. They had a great idea: we could all ride Big Wheels! I loved Big Wheels, and I thought this would be fun! For once, I wouldn't have a three-house limit! I could even go fast!

The idea started out well. As we rode our Big Wheels off across the grounds, I focused on their backs. All was well at first. We laughed, and I pumped my legs hard to keep up.

"Are you coming?" they called.

I noticed that their backs were getting smaller. I wasn't sure whether the growing distance between us was due to the fact that they were taller and had longer legs or that they were "half blind" and I wasn't.

In either case, they soon got so far ahead that I could not see their backs. And we were out in open space. I couldn't see anything but sidewalk and grass.

I guess I was more than "half blind" after all.

Would they laugh at me when they came back? Would they decide I wasn't a fun playmate? How long would it take them to come back?

I waited. They didn't come. Had they forgotten me? Had they gotten lost too?

It didn't matter. I wasn't having any fun right now. I wanted to go back to the dorm and find something else to do. But I had a problem.

I had allowed my friends to lead the way, blindly trusting that they knew where they were going and I could keep up. Now there was no one to follow, and I didn't remember all the turns we had taken.

I got off my Big Wheel and sat in the grass. And all the anger inside me poured forth in great sobs. Why couldn't my friends have just slowed down? Was being half blind so important? Or did they just not think about me?

"What's wrong?" said a kind lady voice. She knelt down on the grass beside me.

"I can't find my friends," I wailed.

"Who are your friends?" she asked.

"Penny and Cathy," I said through hiccupping sniffles.

"I don't know Penny or Cathy," she said apologetically. Of course not. It was only the first day of this program—this program that was supposed to be fun. "Maybe they went back to the dorm. I could take you back, and maybe they'll be looking for you. What dorm are you in?"

Absolute terror filled me. The dorms had names? No one told me that. Fresh tears spilled down my face.

Then an idea struck me. "There's a lady named Jeanie at a desk. She said she would always be there if I needed something."

Maybe the nice lady knew the lady named Jeanie. If she could find her, then I would be at the right dorm.

I have no memory of getting back to the dorm. I did not go riding Big Wheels with my friends again. I longed to explore that open space properly. Next time I would pay attention instead of just following and trusting people who said they knew where they were going. How glorious it had been to just ride! Why couldn't my legs have been longer!

My group of friends expanded that evening to include Becky's roommate. Her name was also Sarah. We became inseparable, and we thought that certainly we would have great fun in class together since we were only one year apart in age!

CLASS

On Monday morning, staff introduced new routines designed to keep groups of blind children safe as they walked across campus together. In those days, children did not have white canes. Many of us would not get them for several more years. Some would not get them at all due to their "half blind" status. Today, things are very different. Children as young as two and three years old are often given their first canes and encouraged to use them in all parts of their lives. Children with low vision—the correct term for what my friend called "half blind"—also often receive canes and learn to use them.

On that Monday morning, my dorm mates and all the children in other dorms on campus were instructed to place one foot on the grass and one foot on the sidewalk while walking between buildings. Our feet were to remain in this position throughout our trek. We were not to pass each other or converse along the way.

Why couldn't they comprehend? I didn't need this insane

method of keeping track of the location of the grass! That wasn't why I got lost! The person in front of me walked so slowly that I could have read a book while waiting. But I dutifully put my feet in the prescribed position and walked.

At the classroom building, staff divided us into our respective classes. That was when the next blow came. All of my friends, including Sarah, were shepherded off to a classroom without me. What was this?

They were all in a class for eight-year-olds. I, who had just turned seven and would be entering second grade in a few weeks, was escorted into the room with six-year-olds.

My teacher asked us all to introduce ourselves. Most of my classmates spoke in flat tones and barely whispered. One girl said in a sing-song voice, "I am six!"

"Please, please, let me go to the other class!" I cried. "It's not fair!"

No amount of crying, begging, negotiating, explaining, demonstrating my reading skills, or standing on my head made any difference. In fact, demonstrating my reading skills had a decidedly undesirable effect.

"You will be a great helper," the teacher said. "We have a storybook today, 'The Three Little Kittens'. Would you please read for us?"

The book was creatively designed. Braille text was interlined with print so that any person, blind or sighted, could read aloud. At the bottom of the page, furry little kitten illustrations were pasted on the pages. The American Printing House for the Blind still produces books with tactile illustrations for early readers.

I read, and when I reached the bottoms of the pages, I turned the book around so that my classmates could touch the furry kittens. I longed for my fat Jack and Jill magazines that had stories for third through fifth graders.

Gym time finally came, and I clambered out of the classroom with glee. Children from other classes were lined up along the walls, waiting for time in the gym. My friends were among them. "Hi!" I shouted.

"No talking," a staff member said patiently.

I sighed.

"I don't wanna play!" Lindsay screamed, hiccupping back sobs. She didn't seem to care about the no talking reminder.

A staff member attempted to comfort her. The more comfort she got, the worse her sobs became. "I don't wanna play!!!" Before long, she was wailing. I sympathized.

LITTLE DEMONSTRATIONS

I was instructed to cut my meat. I complained of pain in my wrist, and Sarah threw her silverware down. To make matters worse, cold asparagus was on my plate. At home, my parents allowed me to stop eating something if I had taken one bite. So, I took a bite of the asparagus. I promptly gagged on the cold, slimy texture and decided not to eat any more.

The rules were different at TSB. I was told that I could not have dessert if I did not clean my plate.

"Ok," I said. "Then I won't have dessert. I folded my hands and sat.

This was the wrong response. The houseparent came around and began to feed asparagus to me, prying my mouth open and shoving it in.

I gagged again. This was the wrong response too. "You will finish your food, or you will not leave the table," she said.

So much for that no-dessert negotiation.

That afternoon, on the way home, I remained in line, but I took my foot off the grass. They could put me in a class with six-year-olds and feed me asparagus, but they couldn't make me walk on the grass.

Sarah and I begged loudly for me to be moved into the class with the older girls; but our begging was fruitless. We spent as much time as possible together outside of class; but even that was not enough. Sarah cried. I cried. I almost tried one of Lindsay's screams; but if it didn't help Lindsay, it wouldn't help me.

The one good thing that night was that Sarah was allowed to move to my room. Penny moved in with Cathy, and all seemed well.

STUCK!

On Tuesday night, several of us girls gathered in the room of an older girl who was 13. We thought that surely she must know the secrets of making it at TSB.

The secrets she had to tell us were about how she became blind: she had been shot. Sarah and I decided this was not a story we needed to hear. We got up to leave, but she found us out. She shoved Sarah down on the bed and sat on her.

I have no memory of how we escaped. I don't suppose I was the heroine.

My parents were still in town, having stayed in a nearby hotel. They visited for a few minutes in the evenings to see how I was doing. I must have told them quite a bit about what was happening, though perhaps not about getting stuck in the older girl's room. I was surprised when they decided to take me home on Wednesday.

I had no knowledge of the reasons why my parents decided to take me home. My mom remembers being upset that we had no toys to play with, that there was no staff person at the front desk, and that there was often no toilet paper in the girls' bathroom. Little boys wandered over into the girls' dorm unsupervised, stuck their hands into the fish tank, and then touched all kinds of things in the environment, including girls.

Mom felt that this was an inappropriate environment for a seven-year-old child to be left in. Many parents simply dropped their young blind children off and left them for the entire school year.

Sarah cried when I left; and we were unable to exchange addresses or phone numbers. I was sorry to leave my friend. I was not sorry to leave the asparagus, the three kittens, or the story-telling bully.

4

WHAT DOES BLIND MEAN?

I was grateful to return home, and I thought that everything would be fine. School would start in the fall. In the meantime, the rest of my summer was spent with babysitters who took me to the park and on other adventures. I loved going to the park and taking walks to Jack-in-the-Box. Of course, there were also play dates with Jill!

I really missed my friend Sarah, and my parents promised to find a way for us to see each other again. I didn't know that it would take a very long time and a lot of hard work on their part.

NEW SCHOOL

At my new school, I spent a portion of the day in a second-grade classroom and a portion of the day in a resource room for students with visual impairments. At the beginning of the year, I spent the lunch portion of my day with my second-grade class.

One classmate spoke to me at lunch; but just as I began to

be confident that a friendship was developing, she moved away. Other classmates did not form friendships with me. I became invisible, sure that I was undesirable as a friend at school as well as at home.

I asked to eat with the visually impaired students, and my request was granted. Lunchtime became more pleasant as I was taken under the wings of older visually impaired students who were happy to make me their little sister.

JUMPING ROPE

In the resource classroom, I developed some lasting friendships and participated in some activities that taught me teamwork. I was the youngest of the students, and I often benefitted from the experience of the older girls. The class took on the task of teaching me to jump rope. Since I could not see the rope, they decided to teach me to listen for the rope to fall and then jump over it. The problem was that by the time I heard the rope, it was too late for me to jump. I needed to learn all of the sounds the rope made during its ark, not only the sound it made on the ground.

First, they taught me to swing the rope. I learned the motions, but I did not understand what to do with my feet. So, they decided to use a different method to teach this to me.

Two girls held the ends of the rope and asked me to stand in the middle. "Now, just start jumping," they said.

I jumped. They swung the rope in time to my jumping, occasionally allowing it to brush my head and touch my feet so that I began to understand the motion. I not only heard it bang on the ground but also the whoosh in the air as it went over my head.

Next, one of the girls changed places with me and became the jumper. I had to coordinate my swinging motions with those of my partner and also judge how high to swing so that I did not hit the jumper's head. I also had to time so that I did not trip her while she was jumping.

Finally, I was ready to try jumping and control my own rope. When I got the rhythm down, the girls and the teacher cheered me on. I enjoyed jumping rope so much that I entered the Jump Rope for Heart fund-raiser and raised several hundred dollars.

IDENTITY AND THE FREEDOM TO MOVE

At school, the man who had played games with the colored flashlights was back. His name was Mr. Reed. He said that we would work together once a week. He had something to give to me, and he wanted me to carry it home after the first lesson and bring it back next week.

"It's like a third arm," he said, placing it in my hand. It was a long stick with a rubber grip on the top few inches. The top of the stick curved over like a candy cane. In fact, he said, it was called a cane. It would take practice for me to become good at using it. When I walked, the cane should swing ahead of me so that the tip was always located opposite the foot that was forward.

My guard went up. How can a person have three arms when one of them is busy holding this?

I didn't like the texture of the grip in my hand. It felt like a giant pencil eraser. And wouldn't I trip people if this thing was always swinging in front of me? Perhaps I could just hide it at home.

The teacher explained to me that people would see the white cane and understand that I could be independent. This I pondered.

I took the cane home with me on the bus. I did not know how to answer the questions my bus mates asked. "It's a cane," I said irritably. "A teacher said I have to bring it home."

"I know," one child said in a taunting voice. "It's for blind people."

I got off the bus quickly, glad that I would be the only child at my babysitter's house that day. I didn't want to hear that word, "blind," anymore.

I went inside with the cane. I didn't want to hear the word "cane" either.

The teacher had given me specific instructions not to use the cane until I brought it back the following week and could practice under his supervision. Well, then, why take it home at all? How was I supposed to get used to it if I didn't use it?

I thought about his words about independence. Just how independent could it make me? No one seemed to want me to do anything lately. Don't walk on the sidewalks because I might get lost. Don't go here and there because I might get lost. And don't run because I might run into something.

Could I run with the cane?

I took it outside and reviewed the instructions. Swing back and forth so that when my right foot is forward the cane is on

my left, when my left foot is forward, the cane is on my right…
Always stay "in step". I got a walking start and all seemed to be
going well. I picked up speed, and down the sidewalk I went.
After about five steps, the cane and my feet were out of step.

I sighed and went back inside. I guess I would never be able
to run.

My freedom, if I ever had any, was lost wherever I left that
Big Wheel.

The introduction of the cane into my life changed me in ways
I hated. I gave up the desire to run. Since I was not encouraged to use the cane on outings with my family, I learned that
my place was at a sighted person's side. I learned to internalize
sighted people's expectations that I should never move around
freely. To rebel against it was to frighten the sighted world. To
frighten a sighted person was something one simply should not
do. At seven years old, I had already become an overly obedient
child. If an adult told me to keep my foot on the grass while
I walked from one place to the other, I did it, even if I knew
that I could see the grass and count the intersecting sidewalks. I
learned that adults' opinions about my abilities overrode my own.

This conflict persisted well into my adulthood and impacted
my self-confidence negatively. By the time I graduated from high
school, I did not expect that I would be able to do much independently, even though my parents and teachers had worked
hard to encourage me to think differently.

I think that Mr. Reed knew that I wanted better independence than the cane gave me. One day when I met him for our
orientation and mobility lesson, he said he had a new device

for me to try. "It's like a pair of glasses," he said, "but it also makes noise in your ears to tell you about things around you. It's called a sonic guide."

The sonic guide was much more than glasses. The glasses were connected to wires which were connected to a battery pack that I wore on my body. The battery pack also had a jack for a pair of headphones which I wore around my ears. As I traveled, still using my cane, I heard strange sounds that indicated things about my environment. One tone meant that there was a glass door ahead. Another tone meant there was grass nearby. The tone might be centered, indicating the grass was straight ahead, or it might be in my right ear to indicate that I was passing it.

Ultimately, I did not like the sonic guide. I missed the sounds of the environment I lived in. I could not hear any of these sounds while wearing the headphones that gave me the sounds of the sonic guide. I also could not talk to anyone. Perhaps most important, the entire device was very large, especially for my little girl's body. I felt weighed down and very monster-like. It was even worse than using the cane!!

Electronic devices have improved greatly. It is possible now to load an app on the iPhone and hear the sounds that indicate objects around me in earbuds that are connected wirelessly. However, I still prefer interacting with the environment directly.

My primary objection to the sonic guide was the use of noise cancelling headphones and the heavy battery pack. I felt that I could not interact with anyone who tried to speak to me as they passed me, and I would be perceived as rude. I also felt that I was a target for bullying.

REFLECTIONS ON SOCIAL DIFFICULTIES

I think that several factors contributed to my difficulties with forming friendships with my sighted classmates. One was the fact that I did not live in the neighborhood near the school. I was bussed from outside the district so that I could take advantage of the resource room. This meant that when school was over, I never saw my schoolmates. I could not run over to their houses to play or take advantage of invitations to birthday parties without a lot of extra planning.

The children in my neighborhood attended a different school and did not see me doing normal things like going to class with them. They didn't have the benefit of being with adults who helped them to observe how I could read and play games.

I developed personality differences that would have made peer relationships difficult even if I had been sighted. I did not enjoy princess movies or playing fashion shows. I enjoyed reading and talking and science fiction. No one put this together. My teachers thought that I needed to learn how to bridge the world between sight and blindness. The message that everyone shared was that if I had been sighted I would have enjoyed sighted-girl things. No one thought about helping me to find friends who shared my personality type and interests. So, I became stuck in a world in which blindness was perceived to be a larger problem than it might actually have been.

One place where I was able to start forming friends was PE class. Because many of the activities required students to work with partners, I was able to talk with classmates. This forced me to learn the names of classmates and ask questions about what

they enjoyed. They also asked questions about my likes and dis-
likes. We learned that we didn't like yesterday's lunch food or
the homework we had to do.

A couple of my partners were just beginning to learn English. I thought it was fun to learn a few Spanish words and teach
them English words they had not learned in class. We exchanged
phone numbers, and they began to call me. When Ana and I
hung up from one of our very simple conversations, my mother
asked, "How do you two communicate?" I said, "We just do."

FINDING SARAH

I had difficulty forming friendships in the blindness community as well, but no one figured this out for many years. People
often thought that I might get along well with another individual just because she was blind. But blindness alone didn't always
make for a good friendship. I was a generally friendly child and
didn't complain when other girls were rude, so the problems
between me and other girls went unnoticed.

I longed for another friend who was blind because I wanted
a friend who could understand me. What I really wanted was a
friend like Sarah. We did not meet again for several years after
I returned home from the Texas School for the Blind. Unbe-
knownst to me, my parents sent letters to rehabilitation professionals seeking Sarah's family's contact information. There is a
letter from a rehabilitation counselor in my files providing my
parents with Sarah's family's information. Neither Sarah nor I
had any idea that my parents or any professionals cared that we

felt so much deep desire to stay in touch. But both of us greatly needed contact with another blind child who shared our interests and intelligence.

Today, due to confidentiality rules, the two lost children's families would have to climb over tall mountains to locate each other. One would need to volunteer their own information and request that it be provided "if you happen to have contact with this child's family." Then the family would wait for the other family to make contact on their own initiative. I am very grateful to the professionals who were sensitive to my parents' requests, and to my and Sarah's chatter.

Sarah and I eventually learned that the same person was teaching both of us how to use our canes even though we lived across the city of Houston from each other. He came to our schools once a week to work with us for an hour. We asked if he would bring us letters from each other. He agreed. We did not expect that anything bad would happen. After all, we would write the letters in braille.

I was very happy to have found my confidante, and I wrote my greatest current secret to her. My braille teacher would not call my cane teacher by his proper name (Mr. Reed). She kept calling him "Mr. Lesley". I found it terribly funny, and I had to force myself not to laugh every time she said his name.

Mr. Reed took my letter to Sarah, and I thought nothing of it. But Mr. Reed was, like many professionals who taught blind children, able to read braille. He opened my letter and read it aloud in front of her.

We decided to get over our mortification at once. We exchanged phone numbers; and when we called each other we identified ourselves by saying in a shrill, nasal voice, "Mr. Lesley, please come to the phone."

I was thrilled one year when Sarah attended summer camp at the Houston Lighthouse for the Blind with me. We joined other friends in pretending that we were shipwrecked in the pool, and I was delighted to have friends who could imagine just what I was thinking!

Sarah thought that I should attend TSB again—maybe even during the school year. "We could be together all the time!" she said. She loved it there. She said, "No one picks on me. Everyone is like me."

The idea struck terror in my heart. Unlike her, I had not had a positive experience there. I associated it with screaming children, being forced to eat things I did not like, and walking around in strange ways.

No one in my school at home screamed, and my teacher never forced me to eat food I didn't like. Something was different about some of the children there. I didn't want to be there.

I would have liked to give a real, fair explanation to Sarah about why I didn't want to go to TSB. I just could not. I had no words to talk about my feelings. The girls at TSB were blind. But so was I, and I was not like them. That couldn't be it. What was it that was different? And what was wrong with me? What kept me from making friends at home? I could not resolve my questions.

I had many questions about what blindness meant and how it was supposed to impact me. I did not want to talk about them with just anybody. If I could have put anything in words,

I would have said that I was ashamed of the questions and all of the feelings that went with them.

I internalized negative attitudes about blindness. I also began to extrapolate based on the negative attitudes I had internalized. This is exactly what happened when I met Kim.

KIM AND THE MEANING OF BLINDNESS

Kim was a new student who came to school in the middle of my second-grade year. I remember her first day of school quite clearly. I sat doing some work in the resource room for visually impaired students. The other visually impaired students (all of whom had enough vision to read large print) were in their respective "regular" classrooms. Someone came in with another girl. Mrs. Richards, the resource teacher, began talking to the other girl, walking around the room with her, showing her where to put her coat. Something was wrong with her. I just knew it. There was something about the way she talked. She wasn't relating to things or to Mrs. Richards like other kids did.

"Do you feel these hooks here, Kim?" Mrs. Richards asked. "These are for your coat."

"Ok," Kim said, rather loudly.

Mrs. Richards continued taking Kim around the room, telling her to feel things. That must be it! Kim couldn't see anything in the room. She couldn't see where the window was or where the doorway was.

After Kim's tour, Mrs. Richards came and told me quietly that we had a new student who was totally blind. "I know," I said.

I loved Kim very much. She was always happy to see me and never ignored me. And there was another thing about Kim. I could help her instead of always being the person who needed help. But Kim's differences from me were not caused by total blindness. They were caused by an impairment in the ability to perform tasks that required putting pieces of information together and understanding complex ideas. She learned after many weeks to travel from the classroom to the bathroom around the corner; but she did not learn to use a cane, and she traveled very slowly.

Kim was unable to converse meaningfully until she was 12 years old. She was able to answer simple questions; but most of her language was made up of repetitions of conversations that she might have heard somewhere else. The resource teacher tried valiantly to teach her to write a few words; but she learned only a handful before she moved away when I was in the fifth grade.

My lack of understanding of Kim's additional disabilities caused me to assume that her total blindness made her vastly different from me. Even after meeting many totally blind people who conversed well and traveled independently, I could not get rid of my secret fears. My doctor had told my mother that I might one day lose my vision. I feared that if I did, I would become withdrawn and grope when I traveled. If I didn't become like Kim, perhaps I might become like Lindsay. Perhaps I would cry all the time and strike out at anyone who spoke to me.

But there were things that did not go together in my mind: Kim. Lindsay. Sarah. The girl who pushed Sarah down and made her listen to stories about how she became blind because she got shot....All these girls were "totally blind." But being totally blind didn't mean the same thing for any of them. All these thoughts and feelings were too heavy for a young child, but they were in my heart and mind, waiting to find words and healing until my adulthood.

NO

As I began to near adolescence, my parents became concerned that I had never met an adult who was blind. Mrs. Richards was a great cheerleader, often saying to me when I became stubborn, "You're going to go to college! You're going to have your own apartment!!!" But her encouragement was no substitute for actually meeting someone who had done it. So, my parents began to search for a person who might be willing to talk to me about life outside of high school.

When I was nine or ten years old, a blind man took some classes at the university in town that was affiliated with the Church of God. He also attended our church for some time. My parents decided to approach him after church one day and ask if he would have dinner with us.

I, of course, was standing nearby as the request was made. I eagerly awaited his response. But my eagerness turned to bitter disappointment as he gave his reply.

"No. She needs to get used to being in a sighted world."

"Why did he say that?" I asked my mom through my tears later. "What's wrong with us?"

"He probably didn't know that you already go to school with

sighted kids and that you've never met another blind person," Mom said. She explained that he was probably just getting used to the sighted world after getting out of the school for the blind and that was something very different from what I would be doing.

I was still hurt, and I saw red. I determined then and there that I would never say no to a blind child's family. I would never make a blind child, or their parent, feel the way that I felt on that day.

5

"I SEE MY KITTY"

By the time I was approaching late childhood, my parents understood that I used my sight for some activities. Although the number of colors I could see was limited, they were useful in telling me when I had reached a room or building that I wanted to go to. Differences in the shadows in front of a building helped me to identify whether it was my house or another house.

When I was four years old, my parents took me to Bascom-Palmer Eye Institute in Miami to see a doctor who had developed a new procedure for treating retinal detachment, called a pars plana vitrectomy. He told my parents candidly that he thought that risking loss of my sight, which was stable at the time, was unwise. The procedure was new, and he thought that it would have better chances of success in the future. By that time, I might actually need it.

In March 1981, the tables turned.

THE CATARACT

I awoke late one Friday evening with sharp pain in my left eye. I went into the bathroom and put water in my eye, thinking I must have an eyelash caught in it. No eyelash came out, and the pain continued. Finally, I told my mother. She called the ophthalmologist, who instructed her to give me aspirin and come to his office in the morning.

While sitting in the waiting room, my mother noticed a white spot in my right eye. She pointed this out to the doctor when he examined me.

I had a very large cataract which had caused a significant decline in my vision. The doctor prescribed drops and ointment for the left eye and shifted his focus to the right eye.

My parents had a difficult decision to make. I could have surgery and risk losing the vision I still had; but without the surgery I would lose the vision soon anyway. The decision wasn't easy, but they decided that it was best to take the risk—a successful surgery would ensure that I was able to see for as long as possible.

SURGERY

My mother tried hard to explain the situation to me. I stoically endured having my eyelashes cut back so that they wouldn't be in the way. On Sunday, March 29, Mom packed up my favorite stuffed cat, "Kitty Soft," a Nancy Drew book, and the Scrabble game and drove me to the hospital to check in.

Preparation for surgery began early Monday morning. Mom washed my face and hands with special soap, and I was given medication to make me sleepy. I vaguely remember being wheeled down the hall; but I will never forget the noxious smell of ether that assailed me as a surgical mask was placed over my face.

I stayed in the hospital Monday night. My right eye was

covered with gauze and a metal shield. Someone decided to patch my left eye as well, presumably so that hospital staff would not assume that I could see.

The doctor came to see me on Tuesday morning, equipped with his ophthalmoscope. Someone would need to hold my eye open while he held his machine, which had a bright light, and looked in my eye.

Things went badly from the start. I did not like having another person pry my eyelids open. The doctor's fingers dug into the skin above my eye. Furthermore, the light from the ophthalmoscope was much brighter than I remembered it being. It sent stinging pain through my eye. I screamed and fought, and finally the exam was postponed until Wednesday morning. I would have to stay in the hospital another night.

That afternoon, I began to feel depressed. I could taste ether, and I didn't like the memory of the mask on my face. I tried to swallow my tears; but I couldn't hold them back. I turned over on my left side, away from my mom and the people from church who had come to visit me. I didn't care if it was rude. I didn't want them to see me cry.

A SPECIAL VISITOR

At some point a couple we knew from church came to visit. I dearly loved Terry, and I even let him stay in the room while I ate a chili dog. I was quite embarrassed about the chili dog because my mom had cut it in pieces for me. But Terry was so cheerful and kind that I wanted him to talk to me.

Terry had amyotrophic lateral sclerosis (ALS), a degenerative neuromuscular disease that caused him to have inability to grasp with his hands and use his arms in certain ways. He saw my hotdog and said, "That's how I eat them." I suddenly felt less embarrassed.

After I finished eating, I sat on his lap. His wife put his arms around me. I felt that I was receiving the best hug in the world while he sat and talked with my mom. I still remember that feeling to this day!

THE OPHTHALMOSCOPE RETURNS

On Wednesday morning, the scene from Tuesday morning repeated itself. I was embarrassed, and I tried hard to cooperate. But the light was so painful! I began to wish I hadn't had the surgery. If I hadn't had the surgery, I wouldn't be going through this now. The nurse bandaged my eye again. I asked When they would take the gauze out. The doctor answered that it could not come out until he had examined me.

I decided that I must find a way to let him examine me. The first step was to get my eye open. Maybe if he let me open my own eye, that would make some of the pain go away.

APRIL FOOL'S

The hospital time was made more pleasant by one person: a soft-spoken nurse named Verna. She was there every day, and I looked forward to seeing her. Thursday was April 1, and I asked my mom if it would be bad to play a joke on Verna. She asked what I had in mind, and ultimately, she assisted in my conspiracy. I suspect that what really happened was that she enticed Verna to play along so that I could have some fun.

When Verna was doing her rounds and approaching my room, Mom helped me to hide so that she couldn't see me. Verna came into the room and made a good show of asking where I was. Mom told her that the doctor had let me go home. A conversation was had about how much Verna would miss me. "I'm so sorry I won't get to see her again. I'm off tonight," she said.

I didn't react to her words. I was busy hiding. I let some time pass, and then I appeared and confessed. Of course, I also got attention for my joke. I, of course, basked in the attention.

Thursday really was the last day before Verna's day off. I never saw her after that day.

THE GREAT BATTLE

On Thursday morning (after the April Fool's joke), I was given a sedative before the doctor came in. I felt sleepy, but I fought to stay awake. I had a plan, and I intended to make it work.

The doctor came in, surprised that I was still awake. Before he had a chance to get near me with the ophthalmoscope, I laid out the rules. I wanted the curtains open, and I didn't want any bright lights. I was going to open my eye today—without help from anyone with painful prying fingers.

I settled Kitty Soft in my lap for comfort. Mom and the doctor complied and waited patiently while I struggled with my eye. Finally, my plan worked. My eyelids cooperated, and I saw light streaming in from the window. I looked down at Kitty Soft. Oh, goodness! Bright, white, Kitty Soft! I hadn't seen that color for a while! "I see my kitty!" I exclaimed softly.

The doctor did not examine me that day. He left, and Mom complied with my request to walk around the halls. I gazed up at the ceiling, counting light bulbs. "I understand now," I said.

I never did go to sleep despite the sedative. Having one's eyes open can be rather addictive—and I'm sure I also felt a bit of elation about winning the battle with the ophthalmoscope. I went home the next day.

UNDERSTANDING

I don't remember the decline of my vision prior to the surgery. Perhaps it was gradual. I do know that the events of that Thursday morning were significant enough to be forever etched in my memory. "I understand now." What did I understand? The reason for the surgery? The fact that the removal of the cataract had allowed for a flood of light to enter my eye and that perhaps this was why the light from the ophthalmoscope was so painful? Whatever I understood made me older, more at peace; and I have never regretted having that surgery, even after *countless* encounters with the ophthalmoscope since then.

> *For now, we are looking in a mirror that gives only a dim*
> *(blurred) reflection [of reality as in a riddle or enigma], but*
> *then [when perfection comes] we shall see in reality and face*
> *to face! Now I know in part (imperfectly), but then I shall*

know and understand fully and clearly, even in the same manner as I have been fully and clearly known and understood [by God]. (1 Cor. 13:12, Amplified Bible)

Without risking the surgery, I could never have appreciated its potential to benefit me. Without taking the risk of placing my faith in God, I will never understand the depth of His love, mercy and grace. Understanding and appreciation often come through experience. How often I insist on understanding God before I experience Him!

TOWARD READING AND WRITING INDEPENDENCE

I had my surgery at the end of my third-grade year. By this time, I was beginning to read and write voraciously. I started writing stories and reading as many books and magazines as I could possibly find. Braille was a great tool. But I wanted to be able to communicate with sighted people, and I wanted to be able to read more books—lots of books.

The writing problem was solved when I was in the fourth grade. Mrs. Richards taught me to touch type. She supposed that since adults learned to type without looking when they learned skills for office work, I could learn to type just as easily. She was right. I easily out-typed the typing training materials. By the time I was ten years old, I was typing stories and Christmas letters to Santa.

I also chose to learn to print by hand. I never learned to write in cursive, but I felt that it was important to learn some form of writing, and I wanted it to be legible. Mrs. Richards devised a tactile board by mounting window screening onto a wooden board so that I could draw and write on paper on top of it and my drawing and writing would be tactile. I could then feel the shapes of letters that I produced, and I practiced until the shapes that I felt matched what I could see when I read large print.

I regained quite a bit of sight after my surgery, and I was introduced to a closed-circuit television. The machine had a camera that captured the image of a page that was placed underneath it and transmitted it to a screen similar to a television monitor. I could turn knobs at the bottom of the screen to change the size of the text or switch the text colors from black on white to white on black.

The CCTV opened some new doors for me. I was able to read books from my local library, and for the first time I was able to read any page in the Bible that I chose—and in a version that made sense to me. I was no longer limited to the few books that had been given to me in braille. I wanted desperately to read and understand the Bible and reinforce the concepts I was learning at church.

Many people with low vision experience fatigue when reading large print for long periods of time. I don't remember experiencing this. Perhaps I was just very patient. Perhaps I was so hungry to read that fatigue didn't matter. In any case, I was sorely disappointed when the CCTV was taken away at the end of my fifth-grade year in favor of a more "practical" mode of reading my school assignments. Braille was not new to me, but returning to exclusive use of it made me aware that my reading options were limited. It also meant that I was unaware of the gradual loss of vision that began to occur during my teen years.

Reading requires use of a particular part of the eye that sees fine details. When navigating in the environment, I used the parts of my eye that are responsible for perceiving movement. I did not focus on letters or small objects. Only when I experienced severe loss of vision did I realize there was a problem that needed treatment. This would not occur for several years. In the meantime, I hoped to maximize use of the vision I had.

During the first year after surgery, I wore a long-term soft contact lens. It enabled me to see objects more clearly and judge distances more accurately. However, one day I discovered a problem. While rounding the corner of my neighbor's house, I noticed that something looked different. It wasn't that I couldn't see the corner. It was that the corner came too early and appeared to be the wrong color. I was terrified to tell my parents. I knew the contact was expensive, and I was afraid I would be in trouble for losing it.

My next visit to the doctor confirmed my fear. I had lost the contact lens. Unfortunately, my failure to disclose the loss had unintended consequences. The doctor and my parents agreed, despite all my protests, that the lens must not have been very helpful and that the purchase of a new one would not be a wise use of funds.

I did not abandon using braille while I was experimenting with the CCTV. Braille was my main mode of reading and writing for my classroom work. I suspect that my parents and teachers expected that this would continue even while they encouraged me to experiment and learn to use new technologies.

I tried out several pieces of technology which were designed to give me new ways to read. I loved these because I could not get enough books! The first device that I tried using was called the Optacon. It was a fascinating device, and I could read anything including handwriting. All that I needed to do was place my finger in a space and run a camera across a page. The shapes of print letters would pop up under my finger as slowly or quickly as I moved the camera, produced by tiny pins. At the end of the line, I moved the camera back to the beginning, down a little bit, and across to the righthand side of the page. The disadvantage of this device was that only one letter could appear under my finger at a time. It was a very slow way to read. I would never be able to keep up with any substantial reading assignments.

In the early 1980s, I received a new device called a Versa-Braille. With this device, I could read and write in braille, and the material was stored on cassette tapes. It was also much quieter than a braille writer. The greatest disadvantage was that it was heavy.

One day, I walked slowly down the hall toward the doors where the buses picked up all the students with disabilities. It was a long walk—the students with disabilities were picked up at the farthest end of the building from the front doors. My teacher's aide, who was with me, encouraged me to walk faster.

I strained under the weight of my bag, which held a couple

of hard-back braille volumes with pages made of plastic ther-moform sheets and my VersaBraille. "Please help me carry it," I asked.

She lifted it and then exclaimed, "Oh! That is heavy! You carry it!"

That was the day when I realized that I would be alone with my burdens about relying on technology.

When I was in junior high, I changed classes six times a day. I carried my heavy braille writer with me as well as whatever books I needed for each class. Since my books were so bulky, they were all stored in a resource room. I had permission to leave class early in order to go to the resource room, put one book away, and get the book for the next class. I did this for a year and decided that I didn't want to carry my brailler from one class to another. It was heavy, and it was loud when I wrote on it. I felt that my writing disturbed my classmates.

During the summer, I learned to use an old piece of tech-nology. I clipped a metal frame called a slate to a sheet of paper and used a pen-shape device called a stylus to punch braille dots through the paper. By the end of the summer, I was quite fast, especially if I used standard paper instead of heavy braille paper.

Later, when I was in high school, I was introduced to a spe-cial laptop-like device that spoke out loud when I typed on it. No one else had laptops yet, but these devices allowed me to do work in my classroom and print it out for my teachers instead of relying on a sighted teacher to transcribe my braille for them.

The quest for the ability to read independently continued for many years. As I became involved in the study of foreign languages, it became much more complicated. I learned that it was not impossible. I often feel that I have lived at the most exciting time in history because of the technological advances that I have been able to experience.

TO PARENTS: TALKING TO YOUR CHILD ABOUT SURGERY AND VISION LOSS

I have received a few letters from parents asking how to talk with their children about sight loss. It is often hard for parents to disentangle their own emotions from their child's emotions. Children's emotions can be incredibly volatile.

You and your child will both feel deep emotions about what lies ahead. But your emotions will be different. There might be important times to grieve together. There are also times when your grief needs to be private. Your child needs for you to give them a sense that you will be with them—even if your answer to a question is, "I don't know." Be the person who will help find the answer. Walk the journey boldly, and your child will take those brave and curious cues about blindness into the heart from you.

I was eight years old when I had my cataracts removed. I think that I would have adjusted adequately if the surgery had failed. I had lost a lot of sight very suddenly when my mother took me to the doctor.

My mother recalls that I told her at some point afterward that I had not wanted to have the surgery. I am glad that I didn't tell her beforehand. I have vague memories of hearing the doctor's words and having discussions with my mom about the possibility of losing my sight. I'm sure that the idea of losing my sight terrified me as much then as it does today.

My mom had a hard choice to make, and she was deeply affected by her perception of my emotions. She told me once (when I was much older) that she was afraid that I would be angry with her if the surgery didn't work. Her decision was guided by the understanding that I would lose the sight naturally if nothing was done. She tried her best to explain this to me, but I could not understand without experiencing the improvement. She had to trust her judgment.

A child who loses a great deal of sight at a young age may remember it quite well and grieve significantly. It is important to give them opportunities to grieve while encouraging them at the same time to discover new things about themselves.

Sight is a very dominant sense. While we have it, we often ignore those four other senses waiting in the wings. Blind people don't really have better hearing or touch or smell. But we are able to pay attention to senses that are overtaken by the sense of sight for most people.

For the person who has lost that sense of sight, I encourage a journey of discovery of all these great things about the self that have been waiting patiently to be found. It is important to acknowledge that the other senses are not substitutes for sight. There are different ways of doing things. In case anyone wants to know, I don't feel faces—it is no substitute for the experience of seeing a face. But I can hear so much love and wonderful stuff in a person's voice that a person can't see in a face! Hearing a voice is an experience all its own!

Most of all, remember that grief heals in time. It doesn't mean that we are "overcomers". It means that we learn to live "with" blindness.

6

MY CAT!

By the time I was nine years old, I had learned the layout of my immediate neighborhood, and I understood the basic rules of street crossing: look—or in my case listen—both ways before crossing. Much of my knowledge came from talks I had with my dad while riding our tandem bike. We covered greater distances on the bike than I ever did while walking.

I was still not allowed to roam the neighborhood at will; but if I let an adult know first where I wanted to go, the adult watched while I traveled to my destination. My independent travels were still limited to within five houses west of home and the homes on the corner where we lived. As my sister grew old enough to ride her bike on the adjacent streets, I became frustrated with my limitations.

One thing gave me a reprieve from my frustrations. During the summer following my eye surgery, I stayed with Jean, the neighbor who lived across the street from our side entrance. Her granddaughter, Amy, was the same age as I was and was also there often.

One day, Amy told me that a neighbor's cat had five kittens. "I saw them," she exclaimed.

I had reason to make frequent visits to the home, and I developed kitten fever. And I loved Laurie. After convincing my parents that I most certainly could find Laurie's house, which was only two doors down from Jean's house, I was on my way to see them.

Someone told me before my first visit that I would probably not be able to touch the kittens because mother cats usually don't let people near them.

I scoffed. I knew about kittens. When I was younger, we had two cats who had litters of kittens. I had been able to touch them when they were still very young. I supposed we would just see about Laurie's kittens. Surely Laurie wouldn't tell me that I could not touch soft kittens! I wanted one for my very own!

Not only did I get to touch them; but they climbed all over me. For several weeks, I went across the street—all by myself—and settled myself on the floor to see what new things the kittens had learned to do. I visited Laurie's house as often as I was allowed. I was fascinated as three of them became round and pudgy while two of them remained thin and graceful. The more time I spent at Laurie's house, the more I became convinced that the smallest kitten was mine.

The rest of my family were dog lovers. I was a head-over-heels cat lady in the making. Eventually, I talked my parents into allowing me to adopt one of Laurie's kittens. On my next trip to her house, I chose my cat: the smallest, most docile kitten. As I lay on the floor to snuggle in kitten fur, she rewarded me

Dad and Sarah riding tandem bike.

by climbing in my hair and giving me a very ungraceful scratch on the forehead. Not so docile after all.

The big day finally came. I thought it was a day like any other. I went over to Laurie's house for my kitty visit and set about the task of locating "my kitty." She was six weeks old by this time, and her fur had become silky.

"How would you like to take that kitty home with you?" Laurie asked, sounding excited.

"Today?" Questions flooded my mind. What would I carry her in? What if my parents really didn't want me to have a cat?

"Yes, today."

Getting across the street with my cat in hand was the most frightening thing I ever did. What if she jumped out of my arms and I lost her forever? She was getting her first taste of the outside world; and she was quite curious.

Laurie went with me, her hands supporting mine as I held my kitten close. At home, I learned the routine of checking her food and water. I also learned the hardest lesson of all: giving her space. That soft fur was alluring, especially when I was tired; and I had discovered the best thing! She made wonderful purring sounds that I wanted to hear all day long. Instead, I had to settle for the gift of a nap with her in the afternoon or at night.

Eventually I settled on a name. She developed a playful relationship with the dog. She chased Brownie through the house and returned with Brownie chasing her at full speed. She became Copy Cat—Copy for short.

The significance of Copy's presence in my life is not so much about anything she did but about the fact that she was always there, sleeping in the same position on my arm every night and hanging out in the bathroom while I took showers every morning. Her presence was a blessing through many nights of tears as I navigated the emotional journey of junior high school. Forty years have passed, and the sensation of her fur and the sound of her purr is still something I can recall. There has rarely been a time in my life since then when I have been without a cat. She did not live long—she died from a reaction to anesthesia when she was only five years old. Some of my other cats have lived nearly four times as long as she did. But Copy deserves her place in my story simply because she was the first.

I was not a good writer at age 9, but I managed to capture some of my feelings in a poem:

When I am alone, I choose my cat
To keep me company.
She is so sweet
With all her blackness
And eyes of pretty green.
When she wakes up
Each and every morning,
She makes a funny meow
So sweet and so warming.
I love her so much
In all her ways,
She fills me with happiness
In all of my days.

Copy was my companion until I was 14 years old. I certainly would have liked to have her companionship for a much longer time, and I felt deep grief over my loss. Her presence in my life made me aware of how much I needed a cat in my life. Since that time, at least one cat has been a part of my life. The cats have played an essential role in my mental health.

7

THE LIGHTHOUSE

When I was nine years old, my parents learned about an organization in downtown Houston called the Lighthouse for the Blind that was developing recreational events for children. I attended the first summer day camp in 1981. This marked the first of many fun-filled years of weekend and summer activities for me. Through these activities, I learned to understand the differences I encountered at TSB. More importantly, I learned that I was not alone as a student who was blind and who attended school with sighted peers. Through those activities I formed some new friendships that lasted for many years.

I was able to reconnect with Sarah in person through this program one summer; and we enjoyed several days of fun in the pool, pretending we were shipwrecked and had to find a way to get to safety.

I also learned to have a healthier perspective about my peers who had other disabilities in addition to blindness. Regardless of our level of academic performance, all of us enjoyed fun with support from staff and volunteers at the Lighthouse. We also learned how to give support to each other. A few of us girls learned a bit of Spanish so that we could communicate with a young child who did not yet know English. When we took a field trip to a movie, I sat on the edge of the seat occupied by a tiny little girl who had cerebral palsy and who could not hold her own seat down. Teenagers taught a little boy to roller skate for the first time. People with low vision offered to serve as buddies for those with no vision without a second thought.

Much later I heard people with low vision talk about feeling resentful that they were required to give assistance to the totally blind students at the school for the blind. I heard totally blind people talk about feeling that they lost opportunities that were given to students who had sight. I never had this experience in any of the places where I studied or socialized with other people who were blind or visually impaired. I don't know whether I was simply unobservant or whether I was fortunate and it really didn't happen to me.

The group at the lighthouse was interracial—in fact, white children were the minority. We didn't talk about our differences. We were still aware of them.

I was old enough to know that talking about blackness was not polite. On the other hand, I quietly observed the differences in skin color between myself and other children when we were close to each other, and I found them interesting.

We absorbed the cultural aspects of our racial difference as pieces of life together. So-and-so's mom didn't speak English. So-and-so walked to the store to buy stuff for her dad, and she was only eight years old. White girls never walked to the store alone when they were eight years old. But certain impacts of blindness united us at the Lighthouse. We all had an unspoken need for friendship because kids at school weren't becoming our friends. The things that made us alike were more important than the things that made us different.

I remained uncomfortable with the use of my cane at school; but at the Lighthouse I had an outlet where I did not need to be ashamed of who I was. Twice a month, I was free to be me, free to run (without the cane), free to reach out to other children in friendship, free to sing at the top of my lungs until I was hoarse, free to swim and roller skate without being told I was going to run into someone—because we all ran into each other and thought it was funny…I was everyone's friend, and they were mine!

Those two weekends a month were welcome breaks from the painful world I lived in every day. They also taught me how to live with confidence. If I could be a friend at the Lighthouse, eventually I could learn how to do it elsewhere. It took a long time for me to learn this truth, but eventually I learned it. Later in my life, I needed to confront some remaining confusion about blindness directly; but my experiences at the Lighthouse helped to provide the strength I needed for many of the changes I made in my life.

THE LIBRARY

When I attended summer camp at the Lighthouse, camp activities ended at 3:00 PM. I needed a safe place to wait for my dad to pick me up at 4:00 PM. One of the wonderful things about the Lighthouse was the presence of a braille library on site. The library has since closed, but at the time my dad made arrangements for me to spend the remaining hour there.

It is hard to describe a braille library to a person who has never seen one. Industrial-style shelves stood six feet or so high, each housing five long shelves or books. At the ends of the shelves, just like in a print library, a label indicated the range of book numbers that could be found on those shelves.

One braille book may take up many braille volumes. For adult readers the volumes can be as large as a 2,000-page print book. For young readers with tiny hands the volumes can be thin like a print magazine.

In this library, there was a real, honest-to-goodness card catalog. On large cards, the title, author, book number and a short description was written in braille. I could thumb through it just as a sighted person could do in a print library and find a book of interest to me. In braille, the information was written beginning on the top line and progressing so that I read deeper into the drawer with my little fingers.

I was a voracious reader, and by this time in my life I had realized that I was not going to convince the neighbor kids to play with me. I often took one or two volumes home one night and finished them within a day or two.

One day I discovered that I had read so much that I had exhausted my interest in children's books. Braille books are bulky, and the supply of children's books in a braille library in 1982 was fairly limited.

I walked hesitantly to the adult books and selected a nonfiction book. This was much better. It was bigger and should take much longer for me to read. I took the book back to a chair near the children's section, afraid that I might get caught and be reprimanded for taking books from the wrong section. The librarian was a very kind lady, but I thought that those "JF" markers were surely there for a reason—probably like the R on movies.

The book that I selected was called *Nobody Likes Trina*.[2] I was afraid to take it home, so each day I put it back before my dad came to pick me up. The next day I went to get it and curled up in a chair to read for another two hours until he came to get me again.

I wondered why the book was in the adult section. The main characters were children, and the book was perfectly interesting to me. Trina had some kind of disability, and her classmates bullied her. One classmate struggled with questions about whether to follow along with the bullying or whether to be Trina's friend. I thought that some of my own classmates should read this book.

I discovered at the end that the book was quite scary. Perhaps librarians thought that children could not handle dangerous scenes in which a child might die.

After finishing *Nobody Likes Trina*, I chose another book. This one was much too big for me to finish, and it was very interesting. By this time, it also became apparent to me that no one seemed interested in my trips to the adult shelves. When my dad arrived, I took the book to the desk and asked to check it out.

2. Phyllis Whitney. *Nobody Likes Trina*. Philadelphia: Westminster, 1972.

The librarian then became aware that I was taking an adult book. The book was a deep psychological treatise on emotions. She questioned my dad about its fitness for a ten-year-old.

My dad said to her that he trusted my book judgment and it was quite all right for me to choose whatever I liked from the adult books. His trust was a great gift to me at that age.

SACRED SPACE, SPOILED SPACE

The library was not just a place where I waited for my dad. It became a kind of sacred space where I processed many kinds of thoughts. I did not know until much later that the librarian was legally blind. I assumed that she could see everything that I was doing at all times.

My thought process reveals much about my world view at the time. I assumed that all people who worked anywhere were sighted and all blind people were patrons of their services. I needed to re-shape my understanding badly. It did not happen until I was well into my teens.

As peaceful and sacred as the library was for me, there came a time when it became a spoiled space.

Not every child chose books—or friends—wisely. Sadly, I witnessed another child interacting inappropriately with a teenage male patron while I was there one afternoon. When the teen was done with her, he began to pursue me. I prayed that the librarian might come upon us and make them stop; but she was busy shelving books elsewhere. I simply crossed the room and hid in the little girls' books.

To this day I wish that I had excused myself and found her so that something might have been done. But I was ten years old.

A ten-year-old is a child. A library should be a safe space for all patrons. It is not the responsibility of a child to ensure the welfare of other children. It is the responsibility of parents to teach children to keep their hands to themselves. A great failure in our country is that safety and security have been placed on the shoulders of little girls who have no power and are often not believed when they report abuse.

THE CLOSING

Many years passed, and I learned that the library was closing and was getting rid of its books. Patrons were invited to come and take books to keep if they wished. I went and selected several books. Some were books that I had fond memories of reading during my early teen years. Others were books that I found in the adult shelves on that last trip and thought should be preserved. They are not all in good condition. In fact, my copy of C. S. Lewis' *Letters to Malcolm: Chiefly On Prayer*[3] is so beat up that I think the spine may shrivel into dust any day. It is still a treasure that I have read again and again—just as my dad has read his books again and again.

To my knowledge, today there may be one or two open libraries where people can browse and check out braille books. When agencies stop producing braille materials, leaders say it is because blind people have only a ten per cent literacy rate.

---

3. C. S. Lewis. *Letters to Malcolm: Chiefly On Prayer*. New York: Houghton Mifflin, 1992.

This statistic has been used for many decades to promote the need for increased provision of braille instruction for children with low vision.

Blind people have always had a low braille literacy rate. Those who read braille desire books to read. We have never had enough reading material. The material we have had has often been extremely out of date and chosen according to what people suppose our interests are. How can we develop more interests without broader exposure to material!

The use of technology will empower us to choose more things to read in any area we wish. However, many of us still prefer to hold physical books in our hands.

8

TROUBLE AT SCHOOL

As I grew older, I excelled academically; but I felt more and more isolated socially as each year progressed. Lunchtime became my least favorite time of the school day and remained so throughout my junior high years. It was a time for socializing, and people didn't seem to care to socialize with me.

THE TRAFFIC LIGHT AND THE DORK

When I was in the fifth grade, the principal of my elementary school confronted a significant crisis. The students in the cafeteria often talked so loudly that they disturbed classes in session far down the hall. Repeated requests for students to socialize more quietly fell on deaf ears—students were probably too busy talking to hear the request at all. A more creative solution would be needed.

The principal had a miniature traffic light placed in the cafeteria, so that students could have a visual cue concerning their volume. If the volume grew loud enough that classes nearby were being disturbed, a teacher or principle on lunch duty changed the light to yellow. When the light was yellow, talking usually grew much quieter, indicating to me that a change had taken place in the light. If we failed to quiet down in response to the yellow light, it would be changed to red, in which case no one was allowed to talk.

One day as I was telling a story, a classmate informed me that the light was red. I stopped talking, expecting to hear the other students stop as well. No one did. Either the light was green or the entire student body had decided to rebel. I knew the truth. "The red light is on" had been a subtle hint. Nobody wanted to hear what I had to say.

On another day, a student asked me if I knew what a dork was. This is probably the first instance I remember that might have signaled the onset of hearing loss that caused me to have difficulty following conversations in crowds. I thought he said "door," and I wondered what kind of stupid person he thought I must be to not know what a door was. Of course, I knew what a door was.

"How do you spell it?"

Years later, when I put the pieces together, my face flushed red with shame. I wouldn't have known what a dork was. And why would it matter…unless my classmate was communicating to me that I was a dork?

MY PLACE WITH THE BOYS

In junior high, I started a new school and made a few friends. They thought my braille books were cool, and I taught them the braille alphabet so that I could write them notes. For my twelfth birthday, a few girls came over to spend the night, and in the morning, we rode tandem bikes through the neighborhood.

In seventh grade, I began taking advanced classes. This meant that I spent most of the day with a different group of students, most of whom had already formed strong friendships. This portion of the day included lunch, the most social time of the day.

Each class sat at a long row of tables shoved together, each table seating six students. The seating arrangement was meant to allow students to choose their seats. They chose to huddle in their cliques.

Classmates often asked, "Can I move you?" so that they could sit next to their friends. Most of the time, I got up and moved— to the next table, where a group of boys were seated.

Occasionally, I felt great anger and wanted to ask how they would feel if I asked if I could move them like an object. I didn't say this. On those days, I simply said I didn't feel like moving. Then I did my best to keep from crying at the table while the girls talked and passed objects back and forth over me.

One day a new girl, Alicia, joined my class. I wanted to get to know her, so I refused to move when asked. Alicia sat beside me, but she was sitting at a table full of boys. The girls who had asked me to move kept telling her they were sorry she had to sit with the boys. I wanted to burst into hysterical tears. Why weren't they sorry I had to sit with the boys?

Alicia and I did not become friends. The next day, I returned to my "place" with the boys and gave up trying to make friends with any of the girls.

AM I LOVABLE?

This year you have been to me
A friend that I have longed to see.
You filled my life with dreams of joy.
Your memories nothing can destroy.
I can look up to tomorrow.
Because of you gone is my sorrow.
When you speak to me each day,
I have started the cheerful way.
In my mind you opened a door
And kept my happiness in store.
In your class my pain is eased.
What I seek is to make you pleased.
Happiness you have sustained.
May your memories all remain.
Gentleness you had in hand
Made my seventh-grade year grand.

During my difficult junior high years, God used several adults who were gifted with encouragement and mercy to minister to me. A few teachers made a special effort to encourage me personally, and this made a world of difference in my ability to tolerate the school environment emotionally. I wrote the above poem because of the influence of one teacher.

I was allowed to leave class five minutes early so that I could get to my new class before the hall filled with rowdy students. My next class was just across the hall. It did not take me long to get there, and each day I left as late as I possibly could before the bell rang.

I disliked the subject of her class as a general rule; but she always gave me a hug when I reached the classroom, and I was seated near her desk. I wanted to stay in her room as long as possible, and I began to enjoy her presentations.

One morning, I became so captivated that I forgot to watch the time. The bell rang, and I panicked. How was I going to get to class without being late?

I put my books away and decided I would ask her to write me a hall pass once the crowd died down. She came over, took my hand, and walked across the hall with me. My orientation and mobility instructor would have given me the lecture to end all lectures—she stressed the importance of using proper "sighted guide" while walking with someone. I should be holding my teacher's arm at the elbow. But her touch spoke volumes to me. It told me that she cared about my feelings. I began to conveniently forget to watch the time during Texas history, and I conveniently forgot about the "proper" sighted guide technique when I was with her.

I think about that teacher a lot; and I am saddened to know now that teachers are discouraged from touching students in any way because of the risk of abuse accusations. I was not embarrassing or unlovable to Mrs. Barker, and I needed desperately to know that! I could never have brought myself to tell her about the pain I experienced because of my social isolation. I wanted to. I even went so far as to end one of my journal entries with a list of teachers I thought I could trust enough to talk to in the event that I ever decided to disclose my feelings of distress. But I could never bring myself to do it, even when the school counselor pulled me out of class to tell me she was worried because I appeared sad. I wanted to run screaming. I was known. But at the same time, I wanted to bury myself in her arms like a baby and sob.

No one could make my peers accept me. Some teachers tried talking with groups of students who overtly rejected me about the importance of peer acceptance. I felt confused about the fact that they didn't want to be my friends. In English one day, one of my tormentors read a poem she wrote about God loving everyone. Was I lovable too? Did she even think about me when she wrote it?

I accepted the teachers' love and allowed it to comfort me throughout the awful days when I was required to act as if I was fine. I was never fine. I was hurt. I was angry. But anger was not permitted. Not for me.

SOMEONE IS PRAYING

Do not be anxious about anything, but in everything, by prayer and petition, with thanksgiving, present your requests to God. And the peace of God, which transcends all understanding, will guard your hearts and your minds in Christ Jesus. (Phil. 4:6-7)

Shortly before my 13th birthday, I became acquainted with a lady at church who had had polio as a child. We talked often, and she told me stories about struggling to learn to walk with crutches and wanting to fit in socially. Once some children took her crutches away after she fell, leaving her without the means to get up and walk home. She eventually acquired the nickname "my other mother". On the day before my first day of eighth grade, she called to tell me that she would be praying for me. All schools in the area did not hold the first day of classes on the same day, and it meant a lot to me that she had paid attention to when my first day was going to be and that she thought about what that meant for me emotionally. When the day came, her prayer took on another meaning entirely.

Mom drove me to school, and I dreaded it every second during the trip—about 15 minutes. As she was pulling up at the front doors, I felt tears behind my eyelids. Oh, dear God, I thought. I cannot do this. I can't cry at school. I wanted to tell Mom to drive away and take me home. But I couldn't do that either. I opened the door and wondered how I was ever going to get out of the car. My energy was drained. Suddenly, I felt as if I was being lifted out of the car by many pairs of gentle hands. In that moment, I understood the power of my friend's prayer. God cared about the pain I felt, even over something as small as loneliness at school.

My lunch experience wasn't any better during eighth grade. I despised school during these years, especially because the more I attempted to seek help from adults, the more it seemed that the blame for the problem fell on me. I was characterized as rude, unable to take a joke, etc.

The "problem" lay in my feeble attempts to assert my need for friendship. Unable to modulate my tone of voice well due to extreme anxiety, I sounded rude when I refused to move when asked. I often did not understand my peers' jokes, which included references to things I had never been exposed to. To further complicate the matter, my peers knew this and sometimes took advantage of it, claiming to be joking when I knew they were not. This behavior made it difficult for me to tolerate sarcasm.

Eventually, I stopped trying to obtain assistance with my problems. I retreated into a world of daydreams during the lunch break, moving to another seat if asked and quietly enduring whatever verbal insults other students sent my way. The school counselor retrieved me from a classroom one day and said, "I'm concerned about you. You look so sad!"

I bit my lip hard and blinked away the tears brimming behind my eyelids. I wanted desperately to tell her everything, to bring my journal to school and read her every last entry. But I couldn't. Doing so would have started the whole cycle over again, and I couldn't take the accusations. Instead, I told her I was fine. I doubt that she believed me; but she could not force me to tell her the truth.

BRUISER

One thing made lunchtime bearable for me. A family friend who attended church was doing an internship at my school as assistant principal. Every day, on my way to get my tray of food, I passed by him.

He said jokingly to me on my first day, "You're going mighty fast! Don't step on my foot."

I stepped lightly on his foot on purpose.

He laughed heartily and said, "Oh, you're such a bruiser! I'll have to watch out for you!"

From that point on, he greeted me in the cafeteria by saying, "Hey, bruiser!"

One afternoon, he called me to his office, and the discussion wasn't so comfortable. He had gotten a number of complaints from girls, saying that I was rude and angry. He wondered if I could tell him my side of the story.

He was on my list of people I could trust. But suddenly I realized that he was on theirs too. What should I do?

The only solution was to do as he asked and tell my side of the lunchroom story. I never meant to be rude, but I supposed that they thought I was rude for not being movable. I just wanted someone to talk to.

I don't recall that a solution was ever found. I remember wondering if he thought I wasn't so sweet anymore. What if I stopped being Bruiser?

When I went home, I talked with my parents about the incident. My mom said, "Can you imagine how awkward it was for him to have to do that?"

It probably was. How hard, to have nothing but hearsay to go on, and to know why I was acting so differently from the girl he knew and loved.

I never stopped being Bruiser. Today, nearly forty years later, his family and I are still dear friends. In the summer of 2023, I traveled to Houston after many years away. I saw him at church—and I stepped on his foot. "Well, hi, Bruiser!" he exclaimed, enveloping me in a great hug.

SKATING

I became hopeful one day when a couple of girls invited me to go roller skating at the skating rink located behind my grandmother's house. I loved roller skating, and I had never been invited to go with friends.

I called my mom at work, and she agreed that I could go. She dropped me off at Granny's house, where the girls would pick me up. I gave them Granny's phone number, and I happily awaited their call.

Shortly before the time for them to pick me up, Granny's phone rang. It was one of the girls, but she attempted to disguise her voice and claimed to be her sister. "Rachel isn't here," she said.

"I recognize your voice," I said. "Why are you doing this?"

"This isn't Rachel. Rachel isn't here." She hung up.

A few minutes later, the other girl called, claiming to be someone else. She had no answer when I asked what she wanted or why she was disguising her voice.

Mom decided to come and take me to the skating rink in case they showed up ready to be friendly. They never came. I felt very hurt, but I also felt that one day they would be ashamed of their behavior. I decided to leave the incident behind and move on, but I never interacted with them again.

ENCOUNTER IN THE HALL

Because my braille textbooks came in numerous volumes, they were stored in a resource classroom that was shared between the students who were visually impaired and those with learning disabilities. I sometimes went to the resource room to work on assignments that required me to access more than one volume of text, such as those that involved looking up words in a glossary. When I finished the assignment, I would return to class.

One afternoon, while I was returning to class after working in the resource room, I encountered a teacher in the hall. Encountering teachers was nothing unusual; but this teacher was only familiar to me in name. She taught classes in the grade level below mine; and this was her first year at the school We had never had reason to interact.

I had been having a particularly difficult week emotionally. When the teacher greeted me, identified herself, and asked if she could pray for me, waves of relief washed over me. I was no stranger to prayer, having spent much of my life in church. Perhaps God would hear the prayer of someone who prayed about my emotional troubles.

I was unprepared for what followed. She placed her hands over my eyes and began to pray—for my eyes to be healed. I had never asked God to heal my eyes and did not know what to think or do.

I thanked her and went on to class. Disappointment flooded over me. No one had prayed for my heart.

Life went on as usual. I continued to search for threads of hope. I also tried to find a place in my frame of reference for the strange experience of having my eyes prayed for. On one hand, I had parents and teachers who told me regularly that I could do anything I put my mind to. On the other hand, I now knew that people thought that I would be better off if I could see. Why was seeing so important if I could already do anything I put my mind to? What about the other things that hurt me? Why didn't anyone pray about those things?

The teacher and I never had any other encounters; and I soon put the encounter in the back of my mind. But having it in the back of my mind didn't make it go away. It only meant that it was gone for a little while. In the meantime, I was busy building my own spiritual life.

9

MY SAVIOUR
AND MY GIFT

While my junior high years were socially difficult, it was also during these years that I experienced the most intense "moments of grace," incidents in which God's mercy was demonstrated in the middle of my pain. These incidents took many forms.

When I was in the sixth grade, in 1983, I began to develop a passion for music. I joined the school choir and began to idolize singers. I asked my dad to take me to a concert; but he nixed my choice of music. I wanted to go to a country music concert. My parents didn't want me exposed to the adult behavior (smoking and drinking) that was typical at country music concerts, and they felt that the lyrical content of the music I was listening to was not appropriate for a ten-year-old girl.

Dad said that he wouldn't mind taking me to see Amy Grant. I had no idea who Amy Grant was. Dad suggested that I try turning my radio dial from the country music station to the contemporary music station. So it was that I was first introduced to Amy Grant. I fell most in love with Twila Paris and began listening to the Christian station just so I could hear her sing. Gradually, I warmed up to Sandi Patti and many others as well. In time, I began attending local Christian concerts regularly.

THE PIANO

I insisted that my parents record my choir concerts on a portable stereo cassette recorder. Every day after school, I set up the little stereo on top of the piano in our living room and picked out the melody, harmonies, and accompaniment to the songs from the choir concerts. When I had become fairly proficient at playing the accompaniment, I recorded my performance on a blank tape. I never intended for anyone to hear my recordings. They were my secret accomplishment. The piano at the choir concerts was so beautiful! Maybe one day I would be able to make those sounds.

Why I was so afraid of criticism I will never know; but I didn't have the luxury of living in bondage to my fear for very long. My mother found one of my tapes one day and listened to it. "I want you to come and show me what you can do," she said.

Despite all my protests, she made me sit and play the song in front of her. She must have told her friends from church about my piano playing. I remember one of them telling me that I wouldn't be listening to Sandi Patti's songs if she had hidden her talent.

I didn't want to play the piano in front of anyone; but I was quite comfortable singing, and I told my mother that I wanted to sing solos in church. I had sung in musicals during my elementary school years; but I wanted more. Another child who was my age often sang in the Sunday evening services...Surely there was no reason why I could not do what she was doing. At first, the truth was only that I wanted to sing. But before long, I had a more important reason for my desire.

MEETING MY SAVIOR

And without faith it is impossible to please God, because anyone who comes to him must believe that he exists and that he rewards those who earnestly seek him. (Heb. 11:6)

One morning in July 1984, I stood out in the garage, having a typical argument with my sister. Mom was inside looking for her keys, and we were arguing over who was going to sit in the front seat during the trip to day care and summer camp. My sister climbed into the front seat while I stood outside the door, holding the towel I would use after my daily swim at summer camp. I was not to be outdone. I sat on her.

She finally decided she was "going to tell". I waited and braced myself for the inevitable lecture about how we should respect each other and work it out nicely. Once, Mom had even made us both sit down and read 1 Corinthians 13, and I didn't get out of it since I had a New Testament in braille.

As I waited, my brain provided me with an image so clear that it could almost be a memory—although I knew that this one was not representative of anything in the physical environment.

I saw a face with tears streaming down. It's probably the only face I've ever seen clearly. As I looked, I heard a voice gently saying, "You know it doesn't please me when you do that."

> *For it is by grace you have been saved, through faith—and this not from yourselves, it is the gift of God—not by works, so that no one can boast. (Eph. 2:8-9)*

I got into the car, sank into the back seat, and covered my face with my towel. I had seen the face and heard the voice of God, and I knew that I could never please Him. I had tried for years to control my responses to my sister's words and actions. I couldn't do it in my own power. As far as my child's mind understood, every time I fought with her, I hurt God. The only way I could please God was by believing in Him and in His son, Jesus Christ. I had spent my lifetime going to church and learning about Jesus, but the things I had learned had been only stories to me. They couldn't be stories now. Believing them meant the difference between pleasing God and continuing to watch the tears fall down His face.

I didn't know much about what happened next, but I did know that the first step was for me to be baptized. I was baptized that summer as a confession of my faith, and I began to think about what it meant to have a relationship with God.

Just two months after I had made my decision, my parents took me to see Sandi Patti in concert. At the end of the concert, she sang a song about Jesus coming back to earth and how we will see him as he is, not as just a man but as a glorious being from Heaven who is the One who saves people from sin. I suddenly understood fully that Jesus filled the gap between me and a God whom I could not please by my own efforts. I wept for about two hours after the concert was over. From that moment on, the connection between music, emotion, understanding, and faith was sealed for me. I understood why I must not hide my talents.

STIRRINGS OF THE CALL

Do not neglect your gift, which was given you through a prophetic message when the body of elders laid their hands on you. (1 Tim. 4:14)

Once I had mastered the techniques necessary to play the songs from those choir concerts, I began to have occasional "jam sessions" with church musicians. There was no holding me back after my accomplishment was exposed. I wanted to sing and even to play the piano, and I wanted to do it all the time.

Church services in the early 1980s were characterized by robust singing and preaching that was full of great fervor. Preachers often employed strong instruction and followed up with a deeply sincere altar call. The altar was often full, and people wept openly. During the evening services there were times of testimony. Following the testimony, the pastor exhorted the congregation to celebrate a happy moment with someone or join a person in need at the altar. The church felt like a community; and we knew that when someone said they were praying it was true. It was not uncommon for a person to send a card or letter, make a phone call, or even raise money for a special need. Friendships and outreach efforts crossed generational lines. At least, that is how I remember things.

In this kind of church environment, I experienced the first stirrings of my call to ministry. Those first stirrings began as simple invitations to use my gifts.

One of the musicians from the church asked me shortly before my 13th birthday if I had ever written a song. I didn't think it was possible. "Oh, I can't write a song," I protested. "I'm not famous." It did not occur to me that Lewis wrote songs, and he was not famous.

Lewis was gracious and did not point out the ridiculousness of my flawed logic. Instead, he began to instruct me in major chord progressions, attempting to encourage me to develop an ability that he was certain was already there.

"If you can play an instrument, you can write a song," he said. I recognized the chord progressions as the same things we were learning in school choir. Could I use that to write songs?

A few months later, I realized that the unfamiliar tunes and orchestrations I kept hearing in my mind were my own songs waiting for lyrics. I began to pay attention to the melodies in my head and pick them out just as I would pick out the choir songs from the tapes. I played them on the piano and recorded them just as I did the choir songs. Then I labored over them and composed lyrics while listening to the tapes. With practice, I began to compose melody and lyrics more easily, and I found that I could even do it in the school cafeteria. God became my friend through song, and He was with me always and became especially near during times when I was lonely.

When Lewis taught me about songwriting, he asked if I would play the piano for songs that he wrote. I was not always good at interpreting his songs, but good interpretation wasn't the point. Getting me to believe I could write music was. I don't know what gave him the sense that I was gifted in this way. I was just a child of average singing ability. But to this day I am grateful for his time and encouragement.

During this time period, churches still had occasional revival meetings, in which a preacher came to town to preach a series of meetings. During these meetings many people often became emotional and "rededicated" their lives to Christ.

In the spring of 1986, one such meeting was held at my church. I recall it vividly because the preacher yelled frequently and asked the congregation whether they "had the mind of Christ," often while weeping. I did not know at the time that I had migraine headaches; but I recall getting in trouble for lying on my mom's lap because I had a headache. Twelve-year-olds should certainly be able to sit up through church and not sleep.

I was not sleeping. I was actually trying not to lose my dinner. I don't think I sat up at all. It probably meant something to my mom later when I said that I did not want Jill to spend the night after all.

In addition to being sick, I also went to the altar. Perhaps Mom thought that all the mind of Christ questions got to me. They didn't. If I was dedicated to Christ, I didn't need to be rededicated. But some other things had been rolling around in my head that I needed to deal with, and I wanted to do it at the altar.

In early 1985, I attended a concert given by Twila Paris with my dad. I supposed that I was the only teenager in the house. But several of her songs touched me deeply and helped me to cope with the aloneness I felt in a world where my teenage peers could not respond positively to having a classmate who was blind. I wanted to hear the stories behind her songs.

What I heard was a challenge: "Stand up if you want to be faithful to Him."

Everyone around me stood up. I wanted to stand. And then I wondered if that would be like giving in to peer pressure—from adults. And I stayed in my seat.

While kneeling at the altar in January 1986, I confronted the sin of my wrong. By not standing, I had been disobedient to God. I should have stood. Oh, God, let me never again stay in my seat when I should be standing, whatever the rest of the room is doing!

In the months that followed, my pastor preached a series of sermons about Moses denying God's call. He emphasized that God would provide if only we would answer "yes." I prayed from my seat, "Lord, I want to answer yes. Please teach me how."

In the fall of 1986, a friend invited me to a youth rally at her church. I went solely because I wanted human companionship. The speaker preached about "committing yourselves to service."

I knew in that moment that what was in my hand, my music, was meant to be used for God's service. I made an appointment that week to speak with Tom, the youth pastor.

"How do you know that God is calling you to use your music?" he asked.

I wrote the answer into a song. It was not the most eloquent song I ever wrote; but at the time I was much more comfortable at expressing myself musically than in any other manner.

> *I want to sing for the Lord.*
> *I want to sing His praises everywhere,*
> *I want to sing for the Lord.*
> *I want to show the world how much He cares.*
> *Sing.*

Later that year, Tom told me that he had a surprise for me. I was having a difficult time with my physical health, and I looked forward to receiving his surprise with great anticipation. The surprise took a little longer than Tom anticipated, but the day finally came.

In the spring of 1987, I turned 15. Tom brought me two cassette tapes, one of which was to be listened to before the other. The first tape began with Tom's voice, saying, "Here is your surprise!" He had read Chris Christian's book, *How to Get Started in Christian Music*,[4] on cassette tape for me. At the end of the second tape, he wished me happy birthday. The tapes were as good as getting a customized birthday card!

It may seem that such a book would be a bit "mature" for a teenager; but his reading communicated to me that he thought I was serious about my own goals and that I would benefit from learning about the music business at that age.

---

4. Chris Christian. *How to Get Started in Christian Music*. Dallas, TX: Home Sweet Home, 1986.

Over the next few years, many people contributed to my education as a musician and songwriter. No one could have known what directions my life would take at the time. I hope that no one regrets those efforts. We all did what we understood was needed in order to nurture the gifts and calling that God placed on my life.

My grandmother bought me a musical synthesizer so that I could experiment with musical arranging. Eventually my mom convinced someone to loan a four-track cassette recorder to us so that I could record my arrangements. When I got my first job, I invested in my own recorder and drum machine. My dad took me to presentations about working as a songwriter and producer.

During the summer following my 15th birthday, I spent some time with family friends in Oklahoma City. While attending church with them, I heard a group of singers from Anderson University in Indiana. I sat forward in my seat, awestruck. They were just a few years older than I was, and they were singing and sharing their testimonies in churches all over the country. Not only this, but they were doing it together! If being a student at AU could offer me that opportunity, then that was what I wanted to do.

I began to sing my songs at church and even in school performances. I was invited to sing at other local churches and youth events across the Houston metropolitan area. Songwriting and performing became intertwined for me as I shared the testimonies behind my songs. The songs were mere pieces of a greater story that God was sharing through me.

As I continued my songwriting and arranging activities, my

uncle Mike encouraged me to submit my work to the U.S. Copyright office. At the end of my junior year of high school, I made a tape of songs. Mike filled out the paperwork for me, and that summer we submitted a packet of materials including a tape and lyric sheets. I felt like quite an accomplished songwriter. I still was not famous.

Another thing made me feel that my songwriting was moving to a new level that summer. Mike arranged a piece of my music for his church choir as a surprise for me. This showed me that adults treated my music as something that had potential; and it helped me to respect my music as something more than just the doodling of a kid. My lyrics were not always theologically mature; but they grew from teenage emotional prayer life to prophetic ministry and biblical teaching.

My participation in other activities showed me that I had additional ministry gifts. I expressed an interest early in my teen years in participating in nursery ministry. My parents were concerned that I not use it to avoid being in church; so, I did it during choir rehearsal and vacation Bible school. Much later, I was a regular nursery teacher for a large church in Indiana; and this was my first piece of educational ministry.

UNDERSTANDING THE CALL

I think that my understanding of God's call as a teenager was quite naive. It didn't get much better when I started my studies at AU in 1990 or even many years later when I went to seminary. Conversations in the dorms and classrooms at AU were filled with talk about God's call on someone's life being to serve as a pastor, a youth pastor, a missionary to a particular country, etc. I began my study at AU with conversations about God's call for me to be a singer and producer.

The conversations in those classrooms always equated God's call with something that a person did professionally which happened to involve religious service. One's life and money-earning potential were all tied into a neat little package, all defined by God before one ever went to college.

Music ministry is a very different field today. Most people work other jobs while earning very little income from their music. Does this mean that God didn't call me to use my skills in music? Was all my development in music, songwriting, and producing a waste? Not likely, but God certainly has a broader view than what I could have understood at that time. God knows what I need and has gifted me with more grace and gifts than I could ever have dreamed I wanted or needed.

I am still active musically; and I pray that my songs are a blessing whenever and wherever I have the opportunity to play. Of course, the music business is far different from what it was in that day as well. It is hard for a person to earn money by writing or singing, and it is probably well that I never put my eggs in that basket. I am glad that people find encouragement through my music, and I am glad to still find ways to use it for God's purposes.

I have learned that God calls a person to serve with their whole life and not simply to serve in a particular way. A person may serve God in many ways through life. That is a lesson that I have learned in surprising and sometimes difficult ways. God calls me to use all of my gifts in service to the community. Sometimes I will be paid and sometimes not. It is a subject for another book.

10

CAMP

I was acquainted with children who had other disabilities very early in life. One child who attended day care with me during the summer before kindergarten used crutches; and we accepted each other's disabilities as fact and went on to have a big time as playmates. Our playing field was leveled when we chased each other around the room. I was slowed down by my need to pick my way around objects; he by his crutches. Every day our shouts filled the room. "I'm gonna get you!" "No, you're not!" We never managed to tag each other. I imagine that many teachers might fear that we were a danger to each other; but the teacher there never stopped us from our game. We were uniquely suited to be each other's playmates.

When I entered elementary school, most students with intellectual, learning, or behavioral disabilities were segregated and sent to one school in the district. I was also sent by bus to this centralized location; but I attended classes with nondisabled peers while most of them attended special classes in a separate area of the school. Observing this segregation had a profound impact on me. The only disabled students I ever saw in the "main building" were those in wheelchairs or with visual impairments—and some of the visually impaired students divided their time between "the main building" and "the Annex." I was never quite sure how to think about the division of students. A child was a child in my eyes; but it was considered "uncool" to be friends with students in the Annex. In the cafeteria, I bit my tongue as my classmates jeered at my bus mates. Yet as I grew older, I found that the students in the Annex were the ones who continued to be friendly to me.

In spite of all these positive experiences, it took me a while to feel like going to camp away from home. Many children go when they are as young as seven years old. I was ten. I think my negative experience at TSB played a strong role in this.

FIRST EXPERIENCE AT CAMP

There was no air conditioning at Texas Lions camp. I sat on the floor, already hot, and unpacked my suitcase, filling up the two drawers I was allotted. Michelle, the girl who slept on the bunk below me, would be using the other two drawers. I was ten; Michelle was eight.

I wondered if I would make friends easily at camp. Mary, my counselor, said there was only one other blind girl. That meant the other girls would all be able to see me. They would all know that I was here because I was blind. Why were they here? What if they didn't want to be my friends? Perhaps the other blind girl would be my friend.

When I finished unpacking, Mary introduced me to some of

the other girls. About half the girls there were deaf. Mary taught me how to finger spell so that I could communicate with them, and I was surprised that one of them became a friend very easily. Ellen was always eager to grab my hand and walk down the sidewalk with me wherever we went—and I was proud to walk with her. She had an intuitive understanding of my need for guidance and was fiercely protective of me without making me feel mothered.

I continued to attend this camp for the next four years. Each year gave me many pleasant memories. One of the girls who was in my cabin during my second year there had epilepsy. I did not learn what epilepsy was at that time. But the girl snored—and many nights the other girls and I lay awake anticipating her snores and laughing. Our counselors tried to enforce a strict lights-out and no-talking rule, but it didn't work. The worst offenders were probably myself and Melanie, whose bed was above the snorer. "Other girls are trying to sleep," the counselors told us. The other girls slept on.

During my third year at camp, two deaf girls led me around the premises faithfully. Another girl signed incessantly to me that she wanted a boyfriend. Unfortunately, the boy she liked was interested in me. The feeling was not mutual, but he insisted on kissing me whenever we met. It would have suited me just fine if he had kissed Amy!

CAMP FEARS AND TEARS

By my fourth year at camp, I had begun to feel intimidated and anxious in the presence of my peers. I remembered my positive experiences; but I also remembered that I had occasional friends in public school, too, until the summer after I was 12. Perhaps the girls at camp would be like the girls at school now. What if they talked over or around me or thought that I was rude?

I made plenty of friends. Carla, a friend from the previous year, had returned; so, had Rachel, one of the deaf girls who guided me the year before. Another camper, Brooke, offered her arm to me even though she needed it to use her crutches. Jenny, who had severe cerebral palsy, sought me out to accompany her on the slow journey to dinner while using her walker; and I considered her a friend in spite of the fact that she could not speak to me. These girls were not like the girls at school. They understood and accepted me for who I was. They saw beyond my blindness and recognized a teenage girl who could be a friend.

The counselors at the Texas Lions Camp were exceptional. I came to appreciate them most during my fourth summer there.

I was moody and homesick late at night, and I had difficulty sleeping. Two of the counselors, Sharlette and Carmen, sat up and let me talk or cry until the feelings passed and I was able to sleep. Sharlette shared with me that she often felt timid and had even felt lonely at camp until she learned that we shared a faith in Jesus. Carmen was tender, almost motherly, and I missed her deeply during the nights when she was not working. Sharlette and Carmen were just 19 and 20 years old, but their insight into the importance of dealing with confusing and sometimes unpleasant feelings was something I will never forget.

The counselors made an impression on Brooke as well. We decided that on awards night, when the campers were recognized for their achievements, we would also do something to show our appreciation for the counselors. We created certificates praising each counselor's most memorable qualities, and I wrote a poem to read.

On Friday afternoon, all the campers in our cabin gathered in the lobby for a small awards presentation before going to the camp-wide presentation. After the counselors had given out our swimming certificates and other honors, Brooke and I announced that we had some presentations to make. Some of our awards were humorous. For example, we recognized Kim for doing the funniest camper impersonations. However, things became serious as we closed the presentations. I had a poem to read.

We're glad to know you,
To be part of your lives,
And what we owe you
As each camper strives
To be a success
In every way,
To make the best
Of every day.
If it weren't for your kindness,
We wouldn't be here.
For it's you who make camp
The best time of the year!

Our celebration of counselors was intended only for our own cabin. Once the Friday afternoon celebration in the cabin was over, we turned our thoughts to other things. That evening, all the campers and their families gathered in an amphitheater for another celebration, at which more awards were presented.

I was presented with my award early in the ceremony and was not expecting anything else to be relevant to me personally. I was feeling quite unhappy about the prospect of leaving, and I was, to tell the truth, enjoying a private pity party.

Suddenly Sharlette's voice penetrated my thoughts. Sharlette, soft-spoken and more timid than even I was, was telling the entire gathering of some 300 people that one of her campers had written a poem...and she would like for me to come down and join her while she read it. Carmen led me from my seat down to where Sharlette was standing. As Sharlette read my poem, I realized that the camp experience wasn't just about arranging fun for the campers. We had given something back to the counselors. In that moment, the formality of my camper to counselor relationship with Sharlette dissipated. She put her arm around my shoulders, tears falling as she read; and I cried great hiccupping sobs. After she finished reading, I made my way back to my seat with help from her and Carmen. Never again did I think that people in positions of authority over me were immune to emotion.

LIFE AFTER CAMP

I went home with a heavy heart, promising to write to all my friends, including Carmen and Sharlette. Once I got home, life returned to normal, and weeks later I sat down and typed my letters. Over the next year, I lost touch with my friends. I mourned privately, unhappy that people who could touch my life so deeply could disappear from it so easily. People come and go in a person's lifetime, and I gradually came to accept this truth.

I was comforted by the fact that I had taken advantage of opportunities to correspond after leaving camp.

One friendship, however, remained a loss thing that I would mourn. My letter to Sharlette was returned "undeliverable."

The Internet has made it possible for me to locate and renew correspondence with some of my friends from camp. Getting back in touch is often a very positive experience. In some cases, it is very bittersweet. In July 2001, I renewed contact with Carla and found that she still lived near another mutual friend, Stacy. She gave me Stacy's phone number, and I filed it away with the intent to call her soon. In August 2003, I learned that Stacy had died due to complications of surgery. Accepting Grieving the death of a peer at age 31 was very difficult, particularly because I had held her telephone number for so long and continued to assume I might be able to contact her "tomorrow." Stacy had not had many tomorrows, and I would have treasured the opportunity to help make her todays happy by being available to talk with her.

In spite of all the doors reopened by the Internet, some remain closed. I may never know what has happened to Sharlette since that summer. I will always pray for her, and I am glad to know that at least for a while I was able to brighten her "today" as she did mine.

Sarah walking a ropes course in a tree.

11

THE GRAY CURTAIN

I took another lesson home from camp in 1985. When I arrived, I perceived myself as part of the "out" crowd. I was different, had some habits that made me less attractive than I could have been and a disability that created a barrier between myself and my sighted peers who were primarily interested in fashion and gawking at boys. While at camp, I developed a bit of a clique with Carla, Stacy, and Brooke. At the same time, I was constantly reminded that I needed to pay attention to my knowledge of how it felt to be outside that crowd.

One of the campers had a disability that caused her to walk very slowly. Most of the campers and some of the counselors became impatient with her while walking from one activity site to another. I shared the feeling of frustration, but I also knew well how it felt to be left behind because I slowed the whole group down. I cheered the girl on, sometimes offering my hand to her as she made her long journey from here to there.

During that summer, I was also reminded how it felt to fear the impact of blindness. For four years, camp had been a place where blindness was only one part of me—and not a very significant one at that. This time was different. Two factors came together to create an experience that I will never forget.

I brought a slate and stylus, a portable Braille-writing instrument, so that I could keep a journal. Nowadays, bringing a slate and stylus, aka the slate, wherever I go is nothing significant. The instrument is a part of who I am. But at that time in my life, I was still getting used to it. I began writing braille on a machine similar to a typewriter that had six keys. The machine was heavy and loud, and it was too unwieldy to take to camp. So, I would need to learn to use a slate, a frame that held paper and required me to punch each dot one at a time with a stylus.

The slate's advantage is its portability. Its disadvantage is that the writer must work from right to left—"backwards." I was unable to master this concept as a young child, but I was determined to do it now so that I could have my journal.

For me, keeping my journal was an act of preserving treasured memories. For the girl who slept across from me, my journal-keeping was a reminder of the direction her life was taking. Emily had recently learned that she was losing her vision.

One of the camp counselors, Debbie, approached me quietly one afternoon and spoke to me about my slate. "What are you doing during rest period?"

I feared I had been caught doing something I shouldn't be doing—rest period *was* for resting, after all. Memories of the counselors' admonitions regarding my friends' and my laughter over Renee's snoring flashed through my mind. I confessed that I was writing in my journal and started to explain that I just couldn't sleep during the day.

The counselor stopped me and assured me that it was fine for me to write in my journal. "Do you think you could explain this to Emily?"

Oh, great, I thought. Now even at camp I have to be Exhibit A on blindness…

"Emily watches you a lot," the counselor continued. "She doesn't know when she will lose her vision, but she knows that she will. She hasn't learned any of this stuff. She didn't put her address in anyone's address list because she can't write to anyone."

Compassion washed over me. How sad to not be able to keep in touch with friends! But how would I approach Emily? What would I say? "Debbie says you want to know about my slate…?" Would she tell me the truth if I said that? Debbie did not give me any guidance. I know now that Debbie was only a college student herself and had not been adequately prepared to help a teenager with a progressive eye condition to handle the confrontation with her impending vision loss.

I never had the chance to talk with her. It is difficult for me as an adult to approach a person when a third party has told me about their questions. It was even more difficult to do this as a teenager. Emily was angry and terrified, and I was a living reminder of what was happening to her. I hoped that she would be able to learn the skills she needed. I have always wondered if she managed to gain her confidence.

SWALLOWED PRIDE

I was chosen to participate in a program for gifted and talented youth at the Texas School for the Blind during the summer of

1986, preceding my entry into high school. At first, I balked, remembering my previous experience there. But perhaps things had changed. In any case, I was older now and more able to speak up for myself if I needed something. Besides, I would have the opportunity to take a cooking class. This seemed exciting; and I looked forward to the experience.

I did not expect to have problems settling in. After all, I had attended camp away from home for several years. What difference would a few more weeks make? I wouldn't even be "camping out" at TSB. I was to live in a small house with four other girls, all between ages eleven and 15. Male students occupied two other small houses nearby; and a supervising family lived between my house and one of the boys' houses. Elsewhere on campus, there were other students living in dorms with more supervision.

Socially, I experienced some challenges. Blind adolescents came from all over the state to participate in summer training programs at TSB. While I had met children from a variety of ethnic and socioeconomic backgrounds at the Lighthouse, we had all grown up together; and it never occurred to us to make fun of each other because of any lack of ability or knowledge we lacked or to compete with each other for status. Most of us attended public school; and we had enough teasing and competition on a daily basis. Some of the students who attended the TSB summer program were also residential students during the year; and others lived in rural areas where they had never met another blind child before coming to TSB. These factors created an environment where often the way that students competed was by attempting to be the most well-adjusted blind person, the one with the most knowledge of sighted-world things, or the one with the most vision. Unprepared for these competitive processes, I was shocked when they began to affect me. Sadly, their effect on me was deep; for at that time in my life, my additional medical problems were still undiagnosed. In fact, they had not even been investigated.

GREAT SHAME

Cooking and related skills were one of the primary areas of focus in the independent living units, where I lived. Each night, two or three girls shared cooking duty; and we all sat down with a skills instructor at the table in the dining room to eat. Following dinner, the girls who did not cook shared clean-up duty. In general, it was a good arrangement. I shared cooking or cleaning duty with the girls who lived at my end of the house; and we got along and worked well. The only problem that ever occurred with this arrangement was that these girls were two years younger than I; and the girls on the other end of the house, who were my age, refused to be friendly to me, perceiving that I was also a preteen.

A more important problem occurred after we had been about this routine for a couple of weeks. My cooking team and I prepared ham and steamed vegetables one night. When we sat down at the table, I set about the task of cutting my meat. My parents and teachers had tried valiantly to teach me to cut meat over the years. I was not ignorant of the process; but I had never been able to explain the problem to them. I learned later that I had, indeed, tried to explain it to someone when I was very young. I do not remember the incident; but my first friend from TSB does. Sarah recalls that at some meal during my first stay, I threw my utensils down and cried, protesting that "it hurts." My protests obviously never did any good. Cutting meat continued to be a painful experience; but I did not cry or talk about it. In time, I simply asked for help. In the case of the ham, I attempted the task—the attempt was required—and was then provided the help.

I had no idea what consequences awaited me. After dinner, I took care of some things in my room and then went out to the front room to use the telephone. I could hear the girls in the kitchen washing dishes. I didn't mean to listen to their conversation; but their voices carried through the dining area and reached me. "She couldn't even cut her own meat!" one of them exclaimed.

My face burned. For the first time in my life, I wanted to beat someone up. Instead, I decided to offer a word of friendly advice. As I passed the kitchen door on the way toward the hallway which led to my room, I stopped and said, "If you want to talk about someone, it might be a good idea to make sure she's not around." Then I walked away toward the bathroom.

The oldest girl left her post at the sink, tore down the hallway after me, and began cursing. I went into the bathroom and began brushing my teeth, my hands shaking. What if she hit me? I might have felt like beating her up; but she had much better vision and was bigger than I. I was not actually in any condition to fight. I certainly didn't have the strength I needed. I couldn't even cut my own meat.

I have no memory of how things ended. I am certain that I was not a heroine. I learned that it does no good to confront bullies who talk about me behind my back, even if what I have to say is true. So, I wondered…If it did no good to talk to authorities, and it did no good to confront them myself, what would do any good?

THE GRAY CURTAIN APPEARS

I navigated around campus easily using my cane in combination with visual landmarks. Groups of trees, buildings with particular shapes, and benches all helped me to orient myself as I traveled from my house to the classroom building, the dining hall, the recreation center, and dormitories where friends were staying. One day, I planned to go to the recreation center with some friends who lived in the dorms to play some games. My route took me past the residential instructor's house, two houses that were located directly across from one another on either side of the sidewalk, under some trees, across a little bridge, and across a road with hardly any traffic.

I walked along, tapping my cane from side to side and watching the trees get closer. Suddenly, I could no longer see them. I knew I was not under them yet—the sun was still beating down on my shoulders. But I could not see the sun either.

I stood still for a moment, wondering what I should do. Something was wrong. All I wanted was to get back to my house and rest and find out what was wrong. I could play games with my friends later.

I carefully turned around so that the sun beat mostly on my left shoulder. I picked my way past the two houses where the students lived and past the residential instructor's house, locating the intersecting sidewalks with my cane, and finally reached my own sidewalk.

Within a couple of hours, my vision had returned to its normal state. However, I continued to experience the phenomenon several times a week. Without warning, the world disappeared behind a gray curtain that I could not remove. The episodes continued, but my complaints were viewed by staff and students alike as attempts to avoid responsibilities. I was sent to bed to rest. When I got up hours later, feeling better, I was not permitted to participate in recreational activities. After all, I had been ill during school and chore time.

I met with the counselor once. I stewed with anger about this meeting. What was so wrong with me that I needed a counselor? We discussed my loneliness, but she said that I was obviously bright and well-adjusted.

Finally, someone took me to an ophthalmologist, who diagnosed the episodes as ocular migraine. Back at home, my retina specialist recommended an exam under anesthesia. I became frightened, remembering the surgery when I was eight. I couldn't bear the thought of the mask and the ether again. I did not have the exam.

The onset of the migraines changed the way I thought about blindness. The retina specialist who performed my surgery in

1981 had discussed the possibility of further vision loss due to long-term complications, and my parents had discussed this with me very openly. I knew that I had glaucoma in my left eye, but I had never thought about the possibility that I could develop it in the right eye. I had already had cataracts, and they had been successfully removed. My right eye, I assumed, would be stable. All I had to "worry" about was the remote possibility that my left eye might become painful and need to be removed.

The appearance of the gray curtain changed everything. I knew that the cause was migraine, but I could not stop thinking about Emily. Memories of counselors' hushed discussions echoed through my mind—discussions that counselors must have assumed I did not hear while I was "sleeping" or writing in my diary during rest period. She experienced periods of total blindness which sometimes lasted for days at a time. One morning I heard her crying as I was waking up. A counselor had styled her hair the night before; and when she woke up in the morning, she could not see it. As the counselor held her, she sobbed and said, "I never know if this will be the last time."

Emily had glaucoma.

I could not get those things out of my mind now. Would my gray curtain someday fall for the last time?

I continued to experience periods of visual loss several times a week during the first two years of high school, usually lasting from two to four hours during the middle of the day. I became used to the gray curtain's coming and going. My doctor hoped that a beta blocker medication would help; but for quite some time there was no difference.

Then one day, the curtain stopped falling. In fact, it stopped coming for such a long time that I assumed that I had been cured of the migraines. I stopped taking my medication with the blessing of my doctor, and I began to push the memory of the gray curtain to the back of my mind. I didn't need to fear total blindness anymore. I would be all right.

MORE SYMPTOMS

During my freshman year of high school, I occasionally became disoriented or fell down stairs and had difficulty getting up due to weakness. I ignored the disorientation and told myself I would have to be more careful on the stairs. However, I became concerned when I began to forget basic facts during oral presentations for my speech class and to notice unusual misspellings in my writing.

My doctor began wondering if I was having seizures and sent me to have an EEG, a special test designed to measure the electrical activity in the brain. It was abnormal; but the abnormalities were dismissed because of my blindness. He suggested that perhaps a sleep-deprivation test would show the activity. Off I went to an adult neurology unit, where I would stay for several nights to be monitored via video, and finally to have a sleep deprived EEG.

My mother stayed with me in the hospital, and some people from the church came to visit me. On the night that I was to be sleep deprived, I had difficulty staying awake, Mom and I played games, and she read to me. At one point, she took me for a ride in a wheelchair around the halls. I became terrified when another patient called out for someone as we passed her room.

In the morning, as I was undergoing the EEG, I became disoriented and burst into tears for no apparent reason. I was very distressed by the episode.

Records from that hospital stay show that I had psychological testing and that I expressed concern about motor weakness. They also show that the psychologists felt that I was not coping well with the stress associated with competing with sighted students and they recommended that I see a counselor.

There it was again. What was wrong with me? I was just a normal 14-year-old. I didn't feel "stressed out". I was a high achiever, scoring in the 99th percentile academically. This did not mesh with failure to cope in a sighted environment. I have since learned that "stress" is often the given diagnosis when doctors do not know the answer.

Some notes from that hospital stay indicated that I may or may not have had a seizure on the sleep deprived EEG. The results were not helpful in giving us any ideas for treatment. A later evaluation from a neurologist indicated that the doctors didn't know how to evaluate me properly.

THE LONG SEARCH FOR ANSWERS

Three times I pleaded with the Lord to take it away from me. But he said to me, "My grace is sufficient for you, for my power is made perfect in weakness." Therefore, I will boast all the more gladly about my weaknesses, so that Christ's power may rest on me. (2 Cor. 12:7-9)

As I grew older, the symptoms became more severe. I began to see flashing lights and to experience confusion and muscle weakness. I had more EEGs, which doctors said were all normal. My search for answers became extremely complex and baffled many doctors. Living with the unknown became a normal thing for me. The unknown also changed the course of my life. For a while this felt like something negative. I have since learned to see it as something that God used.

12

HIGH SCHOOL

The assumption that I was experiencing stress was made by professionals who were unfamiliar with me or with the capabilities of blind students. Academic work had never been extremely stressful for me. My academic testing indicated that I was coping quite well among my sighted peers. In fact, I was performing at the top of my class and should be able to handle any class of my choosing. I chose the courses I took, including whether or not I took advanced literature and math courses. When I desired more electives and had concerns about getting proper access to math texts in braille, I chose a less stressful academic load. I felt no regret or stress about the choice.

My primary concern was socialization. In addition to singing with the choir, I joined some clubs that met before school. Since students were not required to eat with a particular group of classmates at lunch, I occasionally found a group of friends from choir or one of my student clubs with whom I could eat. Having a social network relieved some of my negative feelings about myself.

As my social network grew, I experienced moments of normalcy at school. Students passed me in the halls and said hello instead of teasing me. A couple of students volunteered to meet my bus, all the way at the "annex," and walk up to my first class, in the front hall near the office, with me. I treasured this time together with my new friends. They were older and we didn't have classes or lunchtime together. The five minutes that we had in the morning were precious moments when we built our friendships by chatting about school and other things.

My involvement in clubs required my mom to drive me to school early; but it also provided me additional opportunities to interact with students who had similar interests. This was probably the most important social decision I made during my high school years. I even became an officer of one club during one year, which gave me an opportunity to further build teamwork skills.

THE CANE IN HIGH SCHOOL

My feelings about the cane reached a peak during my freshman year of high school. I had finally achieved a milestone. I was no longer allowed to slip out of class five minutes early so that I would be able to sneak through the hallways and count the number of doorways I passed without using my cane. I was expected to leave when everyone else did and navigate the crowded hallways while using the cane. And teachers were watching me. They reported back to the teacher of visually impaired students regarding my compliance.

Teachers were subtle about letting me know they expected me to be following through when I passed them in the halls. Most simply said hello. Some were encouraging, letting me know they were proud of me.

One was just plain irritating. I had to pass his doorway each morning as I came in from where the bus let me off. "Are you using your cane???" he would intone slowly, as if chiding a three-year-old for staring at a forbidden cookie. When he spoke the word "cane," his voice slithered and slathered as though he was reaching for a grand prize. Friends who walked along beside me grew frustrated with him and asked why it was any of his business.

His lack of respect for my dignity angered me. It was bad enough that I had to use my cane in front of my friends. Being addressed in this manner in front of them was ten times worse—and he was interrupting my precious friend time! I nearly used my "CAAAAAAANE????" to sweep him into another hall!

CHALLENGES

The greatest challenges I experienced in high school often created opportunities for me to learn important concepts and skills that I would need later. When I took geometry, I failed several assignments that involved work with pictures representing three-dimensional objects. Tactile drawings did not help me. I did not understand that portions of the picture represented the top and bottom of the cylinder or that the top and one side of the cube could be seen while looking at it.

My parents spent a great deal of time with me, examining real cubes and cylinders and explaining what they could see. In time, I began to comprehend what the drawings were communicating; and my grades began to improve.

Each year, I had difficulty getting my books in braille. My parents faithfully read to me from print copies of books when the braille copies did not arrive on time. I did not learn easily using this method. One day my mom decided there had been enough.

"Would you please make a list of all the books you haven't had since sixth grade?" she said to me.

"Sixth grade?"

"Yes. And oh, also include the books that other students got when you didn't get yours."

I made a long list. In sixth grade I didn't have a geography book. In seventh grade I got my math book in the spring. That year a new boy started school in the middle of the year. His books came right on time. On and on the list went. Each year I was missing at least one book, and some years I was missing two.

My mom wrote a long letter to the school board, insisting that they do something about the problem. It was a strong letter.

Sadly, nothing was done. However, the experience of working with my parents as readers was valuable. In college, I very rarely had a textbook in braille. Sometimes, even my foreign language texts were not available in braille. I hired readers and sometimes ordered recorded texts from an agency that worked with volunteer readers to produce academic textbooks. My work with my parents likely helped me to develop my skills in listening and directing readers.

BABIES

One of my favorite classes was child development. During the spring semester of my senior year, my class decorated hard-boiled eggs with faces and carried them everywhere for a week. The object of the exercise was to reflect on parental responsibility by keeping your "egg baby" with you everywhere and ensuring that it was "uninjured" at the end of the week. Some students kidnapped each other's babies or drew colored blood on them as pranks.

I decided that I would create twin "premature" babies. Brittany and Holly had little cloth diapers on their egg bottoms, slept in a tiny basket, and went to class with me every day. One day I checked on the basket and found Holly missing, right out from under my nose, while my mom and I were playing Scrabble. "Hey!" I exclaimed.

"You should watch your children more carefully," Mom said, a smile in her voice. "You never know what might happen."

MY FAMILY'S HEART

One morning I woke up very early. I expected to hear my dad clanging around in the kitchen, but I didn't. Instead, I heard my parents talking in their room. My mom was crying, and I heard my name. They were talking about me.

My family was deeply distressed about my ongoing social difficulties. Things were somewhat better in high school, but I still experienced difficulty at lunch. There wasn't much that anyone could do. My grandmother, who edited the church newsletter, tried writing her distress into her editorial column so that perhaps readers would consider their responses to me at church. She wrote, in part:

I have this great idea for a science movie. The main character is abruptly thrust into an invisible world; there are people all around, but they are invisible. He walks into a room that he can't see, wonders if there is a chair he can sit on. He feels around for a chair, finds one and sits—only to find himself sitting on the lap of a stranger. The stranger doesn't say anything, doesn't offer to help him find a chair, just sits there embarrassed. He gets up to look for another chair, runs into a table, knocks over a candy dish, feels around for the door and when he finds it, walks into a closet.

See what could be done with such a plot? There are endless possibilities for comical scenes, and there could be some tragedy thrown in. And the psychological aspects could be explored in depth. Does our hero retreat into himself? Does he find a safe place and live out his life sitting in the corner? Or does he become a bully, striking out at anyone or anything that gets in his way?…

This is not a science fiction plot, after all. I know a beautiful teenage girl who lives in an invisible world. I have seen the people sit and watch her. She walks into the crowded high school cafeteria and wonders where there is an empty seat; no one speaks….She walks into a classroom or club meeting, and no one speaks; no one says, "Here's a chair.

Sit by me." The conversation goes on around her, but she is not included. Oh, someone might say "Hi", but that hardly makes a conversation.

She goes to church and sits alone, no hymnal, no bulletin, no Bible. Except for going to school and church, she is lonely. Come to think of it, she is lonely at school and church.

This girl is bright; she has good grades. She is talented. She is fun-loving, laughing even at herself....Most of the time she is smiling, at least on the outside....

She has been totally ignored by teenagers who have known her all her life. Perhaps they don't want to be bothered or maybe they just don't know what to do. She is different and young people don't want to be different. That's out. To be alike. To be "in", you must be like all the others.

She's a thinker; she doesn't mind speaking up. That, too, is "out." Don't think; just do what all the others do. So, she is different in more ways than one. Maybe being blind has taught her to think differently, and she has a lot of time for thinking.

...People do not mean to be cruel, I'm sure. They do not understand. Our world is not real to blind persons. What can be felt by touch is real. They are alone in a crowded room if no one speaks to them. What they cannot feel does not exist. We make no allowance for their blindness. They must adjust to an unreal world, an invisible world. They

are never really at home. They live in "nothingness." And we, by our silence and uninvolvement, relegate the blind themselves to treat themselves as if they were nothing.

I think we can do better. Parents cannot do it all. They have a difficult task and need our help, also. Parents themselves do not know just what the blind go through. We walk beside them, holding their hands, but we have never walked in their shoes.

Parents ache and suffer along with the blind. This teenager will never know how many hours her parents have wept over her hurts. She will never know how many nights her mother has cried herself to sleep....

I do not mean to put down anyone. There are those who really want to help; there are those who have been good friends and a great help. For the rest, I would like to suggest at least a little courtesy, a little understanding.

Churches were poorly equipped to support families of people with disabilities in the 1980s. Many still are. Better education for pastors about how to talk with youth about disabilities would help everyone to have a more positive and welcoming experience.

13

FINDING MY VOICE

Music sustained me in many ways during the difficult junior high years. Participation in the school choir had given me regular opportunities to sing and express myself. I had begun to write music, giving voice to the personal pain and anxiety in my soul and spirit. Music also connected me to faith; and since I lacked a complete copy of the Bible in braille, much of my understanding of Christian theology came from the music I heard.

The connection between music and faith also sustained my mental health. I struggled with chronic severe depression and thoughts of suicide which I did not disclose to anyone. In the fall of my sophomore year, I began to understand that when Jesus died for sin, he also died to deliver people who were harmed by sin. It was a difficult idea for me to accept because I was steeped in a culture that preached personal salvation from sin. But it kept me from harming myself. I wrote it into a song that I sang at church while I still wrestled with the deep thoughts of self-harm.

For my tears you died
With me you will cry.
And even when I can't feel you somehow
You're always there for me.

I chose to sing that song in a school talent show in the spring of my sophomore year. My mother asked afterward, "Do you realize you just told 900 people you are a Christian?"

I didn't really know how to answer her. It was not that I hadn't thought about it. The song was my testimony. I thought about it a great deal, and this was the reason why I chose to sing it. But when I sang, I did not think consciously about my relationship to the audience. Doing so would have distracted me.

It was almost as if I went to some other place where I could simply sing. Perhaps this was why I could not stand to practice in front of family. I could never reach the other place from that position in Mom's living room. There, I always thought about relationships and performance.

REACHING FOR THE TOP

I participated in both church and school-related music activities throughout my high school years. In my freshman year, I was signed up for one of the girls' choirs at school after the director heard me sing. Numerous other freshmen girls were also there. Each year, the director auditioned us again and placed us all in the choir where we were most suited based on our abilities.

I dreamed of singing with the Chorale, the mixed choir which represented the best voices in the school. Every day I practiced after school in my room, singing anything I could think of. But each year I remained with the girls' choir.

I became frustrated, noting that none of my hard work seemed to change the reason given to me each year as an explanation: "You aren't ready." Every year, I cried and vowed to work harder; but I didn't know what to work on. I practiced for hours each afternoon, learning not only my part but all the other parts to the choir music. I learned to play the choir songs on the piano. I learned to sing all kinds of music. I had perfect pitch; but I struggled with chronic respiratory problems which made my voice weak and raspy…ugly, I thought. Perhaps voice lessons would help.

THE SEARCH FOR MY VOICE

My first private voice teacher was a fine teacher, but his style did not match my needs. Try as I might, I could not master the concept of "head voice". My high notes squeaked, and my voice was thin. This was worse than the original problem. And apparently, I wasn't the only one who noticed.

I participated in an annual solo and ensemble contest every year between seventh and ninth grades. Performances were scored from 1 to 3 with 1 meriting the singer a medal. Each year, I brought home medals for both my solo and ensemble performances. I looked forward to participating again during my sophomore year, singing a piece that was more challenging.

I worked hard with my teacher's assistance, memorizing the

piece and becoming confident about the notes. When the day came, people went into the contest rooms to sing their pieces one after the other. Then everyone congregated in the cafeteria to wait for scores to be posted. We congratulated each other when 1s were posted.

Then my score was posted: a 2. My friend, Kevin, read it softly to me and said gently, "I'm sorry, Sarah." I broke into great sobs; and he wrapped his arms around me. "I don't respect you any less," he said.

The rating didn't matter; but my singing did. Something had happened to my voice. I was quite aware of the change; and I did not know what to do.

The girls' choir took a trip that spring. While on the trip, I confided in the director about my frustration.

After some time, she sat down with me beside a river's edge and spoke words I will never forget. "I don't know what your teacher is doing with you," she said, "but it is ruining your voice. If you don't stop it, you will develop nodes on your vocal chords."

Vocal nodes were a terribly dreaded thing. All of us girls had heard stories about how our choir director had undergone treatment for them and could not sing for some time. Her words terrified me; and I had no reason to distrust her. I would have to find some other way to accomplish what I needed to do. I could not risk vocal nodes. Singing was too important to me.

During the summer following my sophomore year of high school, the choir director offered a six-week course of individualized voice lessons. I signed up, eager to take advantage of her assistance. We worked hard to undo some of the damage done by the techniques I had developed during my previous lessons.

I was working as a receptionist that summer, and we used my work as a voice development project. Answering the phone became an opportunity for me to practice relaxing while using my voice. I had never realized how tense I was when I spoke and sang. The more I practiced, the more I began to notice improvement. Respiratory problems still plagued me; but I noticed the tension returning when I became excited or frightened. I even began to be able to speak while crying, something I had not been able to do before because of the intense constriction of my throat.

During my junior year, I began taking lessons from another voice teacher. Jennie was a student pursuing her Master's degree at a local university. Our lessons were very relaxed, and she often told stories or conversed to build rapport with me. She used that rapport to make her points. During one lesson, she stopped me in the middle of a song. "You're too timid," she said. "These people are stupid. You've got something to say, and you've got to make them listen to you!" She encouraged me to think of my own songwriting, to use this perspective to connect with the lyrics to the songs that I was singing, and to use my own pain as a resource when I sang.

I had never thought of this idea. I had always put a lot of strength into pushing my pain away, protecting people from it. I understand now that this probably fueled many of my vocal difficulties.

I began to lean into the lyrics of the music, even if my interpretations were different from the intended interpretations. My voice began to relax, and I sang freely.

THE CONFRONTATION

When the Chorale list was posted at the end of my junior year, I was not surprised to find that I wasn't on it. I didn't expect anything to change, but I needed to know the truth. A fear had been growing in my mind. Every spring, the choral groups participated in a contest which involved performing three previously rehearsed pieces and sight reading a piece which they had never seen before. I participated in the choral performances with the girls' choir but always sat out for the sight-reading portion. I began to wonder if my inability to sight read was the reason I had never been selected to sing with the Chorale.

I knew the risks of asking. I might never learn the truth. If I did, I would be deeply hurt. But I had to know.

I asked my mother to drive me to school early one morning so that I could speak to the director of the Chorale. I only remember one thing about the meeting: his hesitant confession that my inability to sight read was, indeed, the problem.

Deeply hurt, I thought of little else throughout the day. The truth was that I could indeed sightread. Before I had ever attempted to play choral pieces by ear, I had tried to learn to play the piano using braille music. The first six months were moderately successful. However, my sighted piano teacher did not know braille; and no one else in my life knew anything about braille music. Frustrated by the inability to figure out unfamiliar signs, I stopped taking piano lessons.

Seven years had passed, though; and I wondered whether I might be more successful at reading braille music at this point in my life now that I had general music knowledge and better thinking skills. Surely it was worth a try.

I spoke with the director of the girls' choir. She became excited, as if a light had gone on. "We should have braille music for you," she said.

THE SIGHT-READING CONTEST

The teacher of visually impaired students labored over the summer to learn both print and braille music so that she could provide my pieces for use in class. In September, I took my place among the other members of the Chorale and read from my own copy of the music. I not only read from my own copy during rehearsals; but I also participated in weekly sight-reading tests and scored very well.

In the spring, I participated for the first time in the sight-reading portion of the UIL contest. The most difficult part of the task required me to read words and notes at the same time. For a sighted person, perhaps this is not so challenging. For a blind person, it can be nearly impossible to follow two lines at once. I developed a method of reading over the words quickly during the study time so that I could use my less dominant finger to follow them while concentrating more heavily on the notes during the performance.

The sightreading music at the UIL contest presented a challenge to me that was never presented to my classmates. The key signature was written incorrectly in my music. We used our first minute to study the notation before singing the piece using "sol fege" syllables (do, re, mi…). When we began singing, I panicked. I was singing the wrong syllables!

I skimmed my music, trying to determine if I was in the wrong place. I wasn't. I was reading the same notes that everyone else was reading—I recognized the pitches. It was then that I discovered the mistake in the key signature. In my mind, I threw it out and replaced it with the correct one, reading the notes as they should have been read, converting them using the intervals.

THE REAL VOICE LESSON

And whatever you do, whether in word or deed, do it all in the name of the Lord Jesus, giving thanks to God the father through him. (Col. 3:17)

The fact that I sang with the Chorale doesn't matter so much now that high school is far behind me. Yet it mattered to me then and it was the yardstick I used to measure my vocal abilities. I dreamed of someday singing and playing my songs as a ministry; and although I knew that God's call was the most important factor in whether or not such an opportunity would arise for me, I also knew that developing my talent was important. Had I not confronted the director with my questions, I would have missed the opportunity to learn what I could do— and probably an opportunity to grow as well.

The incident with the Chorale was my first real taste of what it feels like to be denied an opportunity because of my disability.

Finding a balance between standing up for what is right and fighting a battle simply for the principle behind the victory is difficult. God has granted us, His creation, with freedoms—and one of those is the freedom to judge one another. Often, we use inappropriate and even unfair criteria to evaluate each other's worth or ability to contribute to what a group is doing. From that early experience, I learned that sometimes doors which God is willing to open can be blocked by the judgments of other people and assumptions about the availability of resources. Deciding on the best method for getting through or around those blocks is a matter which requires courage as well as faith, perseverance, and humility. Without these things, I could not have carried on and worked to prove that I had the qualities I needed to participate equally. The experience was painful to me as a teenager, but it helped me to develop skills I would need later.

During the summer of 1989, just before the beginning of my senior year, my family traveled to Anderson and met briefly with some staff and faculty. During those meetings, I discovered that AU offered a degree in music business. As part of this degree, I could take courses in choral arranging and music production among other things. I had been writing songs for several years; and by this time, I had already experimented with home recording and had arranged a few songs in parts. How exciting! I could be in class learning to do more of what I already loved. I arranged to visit the school again during the fall so that I could find out what college life was like.

I returned to Anderson in September and spent a weekend with a friend who was a freshman. I slept on the floor in her dorm room, ate in the cafeteria with her, and attended a couple of classes. I tagged along to impromptu gatherings in other girls' dorm rooms and was welcomed with open arms. This was the kind of college experience I wanted.

In January 1990, my acceptance letter finally came. Orientation would be held in April and August. My father and I made plans to attend the session in April. By the end of the weekend, I had my fall schedule in hand.

My parents planned a creative graduation party for me. They invited as many of the students from my original resource room group as they could contact as well as one of my first teachers. Some friends from church and some neighbors also attended. Everyone signed their name in puffy paint on a huge card so that I could read it. Cake was eaten and gifts given, and I began to anticipate the changes that would take place that fall.

14

THE VALLEY OF TEARS

My maternal grandparents, Granny and Gramps, were faithfully present throughout my childhood and teen years. I took for granted that they would be there forever. Almost every day I called them and each week I saw them at church. When my mother played the piano, I often sat with them.

They became everyone's adopted grandparents. My peers all called them Granny and Gramps. Granny handed out little sticks of gum to any child who asked. She had an infectious laugh in which she opened her mouth wide and cackled happily.

SCATTERED MEMORIES

Granny loved sewing crafts and put her gifts to good use for my sister and me. She made us dolls to play with when we were children. She also made us clothes to wear for ourselves. When I was in high school, girls wore dresses with bubbles in the skirts and bubbles in the sleeves. Granny's birthday gifts to me were often new dresses or skirts, sometimes partially finished because she needed a last measurement.

When I was a teenager, Granny bought a new thing: a cassette deck with a player on one side and a recorder on the other side so that copies of tapes could be made. She allowed me to use it heavily, and I made hundreds of tapes with various combinations of songs. I also made copies of my written music for other people to keep.

The cassette deck was heavy and very noticeable. She hauled it to my choir concerts to make recordings. She was careful to start recording just when the choir took the stage and to pause when one choir left and another went onstage. Knowing how much I loved hearing the music again and again, she didn't limit her recordings to my choir alone.

Granny taught me to play Scrabble and Uno when I was seven years old. I cried when Gramps gave me my first draw 4 card. She put me on her lap, let me cry all my tears and talk about how I thought it wasn't fair that I had such a huge card pile, and talked to me gently about how in the game of Uno this happened sometimes and I would get a chance soon to give Gramps a draw 4. (She was right.)

She won all of the Scrabble games and did not share her secret to memorizing seven-letter words. She loved to play other types of games as well, including games with colored pieces that I could not see. The number of games that were accessible to me at the time was very limited. She never complained when we were at a large family reunion and I needed someone to play Scrabble with me.

Our church made heavy use of its hymnal, and I can recall the sound of strong four-part harmony resounding from all over the sanctuary. I had no hymnal in braille, and this bothered a number of people. On one day, a little girl who sat next to me took my hand, placed it on her print hymnal, and exclaimed, "Sing!!!"

Granny decided to record the lyrics to our most frequently-sung hymns for me. She introduced her project by saying, "I want you to put your headphones on so that your mother can't hear me. There will be no laughing, no snickering, no jokes about old people, etc." She began each new hymn by singing the first verse and chorus and then dictated all of the lyrics. She apologized profusely for singing off key, but every note was in perfect pitch.

When she got tired of singing, she took a break and read me funny stories from the Reader's Digest magazine. Once when she got ready to read her chosen *Reader's Digest* passage, she asked, "Are you tired of brailling yet?"

As she flipped her pages and decided what to read or sing, she sang nonsense syllables: "Lu-la-lu'lu'lu'lu! Oh, you'll enjoy this little joke!" or "Here's a good one!" I never knew whether she was flipping pages in the magazine or the hymnal until she started singing or reading.

My one regret is that I was too embarrassed to sing in front of Granny. She wanted strongly to give me voice lessons herself. My family and teachers had criticized me, often as constructively as possible, about my tendency to make faces while singing. Every time I sang, I heard numerous people in my memory, saying, "Don't make faces!" I could not bring myself to stand in front of Granny and allow her to look at my face while I tried to sing beautiful high notes. Today, knowing the reason why I could not sing those notes and hearing sounds come from me that are so much like her, I am sorry that we did not have the knowledge then that would have made me free to sing with her.

THE TRIP

During the summer before my sophomore year, Granny and Gramps took me on a long cross-country trip. We made stops in several states to visit family and friends. We first stopped in Oklahoma to visit Granny's old friend Helen. When we arrived, Helen banished the man to the living room and invited me and Granny to the kitchen to chat.

"Oh, something smells wonderful!" I exclaimed.

"What do you think it is?" Helen asked.

"It smells delicious, like biscuits!" I said.

"Biscuits!" she cried "Do you think you came all the way here for biscuits?"

She refused to disclose what she was cooking until after dinner. The men had heard me say the word biscuits, and they asked over and over when the biscuits would be served. After dinner I learned that there was a nice, fresh apple pie for us. I think the men knew all about it.

From Oklahoma, we drove to Colorado to spend some time with My aunt and uncle and cousins. I remember little of my time in Colorado except that it was there that I saw lightning for the first time. It was both fascinating and terrifying to see it streaking across the sky.

Our next stop was in Nebraska for a family reunion. Most of the family had not seen me since I was very little, so I didn't remember them. I had a good time anyway.

After the stop in Nebraska, we went on to Minnesota to visit Gramps' sisters. Along the way, Granny became very hungry for rhubarb pie. "Surely there's a restaurant around here that serves rhubarb pie!" she complained. "This is North Dakota!"

We stopped at several places just to ask whether they served rhubarb pie. When we finally found a place that served it, we also found that it was not very clean. When we left, Granny said, "I wonder what your mom would think if I told her we ate in a dirty basement."

Minnesota was about as different from Houston as it was possible to get. There was no air conditioning. Granny washed out clothes in a ringer washer. I asked if I could see it and then yanked my hands away at its oily texture and wondered how such a thing could clean one's clothes.

Granny forgot to tell me that the house where we stayed was across the street from a train track. Every night at midnight, a train came roaring past the house. On the first night, I sat bolt upright, remembering that someone told me that a tornado would sound like a train.

Granny had heard the train coming and had come into my room, knowing that I would wake up. She lay down and rubbed my back until I fell asleep.

Knowing the train was there didn't make it any better the

second night. Granny had to put her 15-year-old granddaughter back to bed every night until we left.

THE BEGINNING OF LOSS

I don't remember much about my junior year of high school. Therapists might tell me this is because it was a traumatic year. Well, I suppose it was. Perhaps the most important mark of trauma is the tendency to think of it as no big deal, even to not talk about it.

I remember two things in particular. In the fall, I made a deliberate decision not to tell my parents about the return of my neurological symptoms. I experienced several episodes of confusion and slurred speech during the summer of 1988 which were witnessed by adults. One occurred while I was finishing a voice lesson. My teacher encouraged me to sit down in a soft, overstuffed chair and brought me a glass of water. I was not fully recovered when my mom arrived to pick me up.

"What's wrong?" Mom asked as I got in the car.

I tried to hide the episode, remembering the recommendations following my hospitalization. She recognized it and my journal indicates that she mentioned the possibility of taking me to a psychologist. Seeing a psychologist was an absolute terror for me. So, I did not discuss my problems anymore.

I fell down stairs several times and experienced slurred speech often, but I did not want more counseling. So, I ignored the episodes that occurred while I was at school. As long as no one witnessed them or talked to my parents about them, I wouldn't have to go to the psychologist. I could blame the falling on accidents. I didn't like it, but it was better than having a psychologist blame this on not being able to handle a sighted school—or, worse, telling me I was fine, and they didn't know what to do. If I was fine, then I didn't need a psychologist anyway.

In the spring, Granny was diagnosed with breast cancer. She had surgery, and at the time her treatment was considered successful. But I was very frightened and could not put my fears in words. Beyond that, I felt that people might think I was being overdramatic or that people might think I was seeking attention for myself. So, I tried to be tough and go back to school.

At school there was a problem. We were taking senior pictures, and I hadn't known anything about it. If I had known, I would have worn a nice dress. I was wearing jeans and the first shirt I pulled out that morning. And I couldn't smile.

A nice girl named Brittany stood next to me for the group picture and gave me directions about where the camera was. I was very grateful since we had never even met. I wished that I could go back in time and meet her in my past. Maybe we could have been friends, especially if I could have been cheerful.

I tried very hard to smile for the pictures, but I just couldn't. The best I could do was look in the right direction.

The worst was yet to come. There were individual pictures. Samantha, a friend from the journalism class, was helping with the photo shoots. "Smile!" she encouraged. She even sounded encouraging, not fake like people in a store photo shoot.

I just couldn't smile. By the third attempt, I was crying. Samantha hugged me. "Are you ok?" she asked. I could tell she meant it.

Sarah and Granny at high school graduation.

No matter how hard I tried, I couldn't stop the tears. I shook my head and told her what happened. She hugged me tight and let me go. "We can just do it another day."

I went off to French class by way of the bathroom. I splashed water on my face, then pumped powdery soap into my hand and rubbed my hands together until it dissolved. I wished there were more things I could do before going to class.

I was late to class. I sat in my desk as quietly as possible, unzipped my bag, and took out my French book. I tried to concentrate. All was well until my teacher called on me. Then it happened again. The big lump came back up my throat, and I couldn't answer her question.

"Are you ok?" my teacher asked.

I shook my head.

"What's wrong?" she asked.

I couldn't answer. I opened my mouth and no words came.

"Do you just not want to be here?" she asked gently.

I shook my head violently, throwing my book into my bag and going into the hall. Standing in the hall, I shook with silent sobs.

She came out and took me to the teacher's lounge, where she helped me to call my parents. Someone came to get me and took me to the hospital, where I could be with the family. Eventually, I went home because I was running a fever. I spent the next several days sleeping.

My parents were always open with me about my own medical history, but I was afraid to ask questions about what was happening to Granny. I am certain that had I asked, they would have been as honest with me as they could. I wanted to ask,

"Will Granny die?" At the same time, I knew that all was being done so that she would live. I did not know how to cope with the dichotomy of emotions brutalizing my heart or even how to put them in words. They simply poured out in tears until my body could find a way physically to cope with what I could not express.

Mom took me to the hospital to be with the family. Later that afternoon, I went home to sleep. I was, in fact, not ready to go back to school. I was running a temperature of 102. I slept and ran fever for the next four days.

In time, we all settled back into family routines again. We didn't talk much about breast cancer anymore. We treated it as if it was gone. That gave us the freedom to appreciate the time we had. It also left us unprepared for what came later.

15

WORK, HOPES, AND DREAMS

During the summer of 1988, after I turned 16, I participated in a job training experience for teenagers sponsored under the Job Training Partnership Act. I was very excited as I sat in the orientation with Michelle, a friend from school who was another disabled student. Both of us felt a special kind of pride on this day.

In this program, we participated along with nondisabled peers. We were not singled out as people with disabilities who needed special training. Neither of us had a special teacher. We were recognized as people who could work in jobs just like our peers.

All of us were asked to specify what types of jobs we were interested in. Since I had been volunteering in the church nursery for several years and had some interest in teaching, I said that I would like to work in a day care. Michelle also wanted to work at a day care. We hope that maybe we might get to work together.

We didn't. Michelle got to work at a day care. I was placed as a receptionist—at the Commission for the Blind. I felt that I had been sent there because I was blind and that perhaps some-one thought that I could not work anywhere else.

When I asked the JTPA counselor about this, she said that the Commission had requested a blind teenager to work at the office. I had many doubts but decided to make it a success.

The Commission provided me with training materials to listen to about how to provide good customer service. As things happened, I was able to use the work as part of my voice training. I learned to speak correctly, and this had a significant impact on my singing.

I enjoyed using my earnings for things that were important to me. I bought some musical equipment, and I paid veterinary expenses for a stray cat that I decided to keep.

A FRIEND

My supervisor stressed to me that I must never fraternize with callers or take any personal calls at the office unless I was on a break. I did my best to follow the rules faithfully. There was a great deal of time during the day when no calls came in. I had a small electronic device with a little bit of memory and a laptop-style keyboard. Laptops were not widely popular at that time and certainly were not accessible to people who were blind. This small note-taking device allowed me to write notes to myself, take messages for people at work and print them out, and keep a journal. I spent the time writing and not taking personal calls.

But one day a caller seemed determined to make me break those rules. She called and requested to speak with the office manager. He was out for the day, so I asked if I could take her message.

"Oh, are you the new little girl!" she exclaimed in a raspy voice. She sounded happy to hear my voice, and I supposed that Jerry had told her I was coming. But I had to find a way to get off that phone!

"Yes, I am, but…"

"Oh, you sound so lovely! My name is Elaine Johnson." She continued to talk, lavishing love on me and sounding as if she might continue all day.

After about ten minutes, I thanked her warmly and said, "I will be sure that Jerry knows your message is on his desk first thing in the morning."

I did not know at the time that Jerry was suffering with advanced complications of polio. He was rarely in the office for the following weeks, and he died that summer.

Elaine called frequently to ask whether I knew how he was doing. I never knew, and the office staff protected me from the details of his condition.

Since I did not know Jerry personally, I was not deeply affected by his death. Elaine was his friend, and she grieved deeply. She made it her mission to have me as a young friend, and she often followed up her questions about Jerry with questions about how I was getting along in the office. I felt very panicky at this point, remembering my supervisor's stern admonishment about not taking personal calls. "Oh, it's all right," Elaine said, almost in a whisper. "Listen, if anyone is not nice to you, you let me know and I'll take care of it."

At some point she gave me her telephone number. In my mind I heard my mother's voice, telling me not to bother her too much. But my heart heard the sound of Elaine's voice, so sad as I told her that I needed to go and take calls. In the evening when I got home, I picked up my home phone and dialed her number. Instead of great sadness, I heard a smile. She asked me numerous questions about my life, my singing, how I liked working at the Commission, etc. I told her about a coworker whose smoking in the office was bothering me, and she exclaimed about how Jerry would never have permitted smoking in the office if he had been there.

We began to have regular conversations, and I felt that perhaps we both enjoyed them. I tried not to call too often, but I also learned that Elaine wasn't well herself. I called and checked on her every few weeks. It seemed to give her great joy to pour goodness into me. Her friendship became deeply meaningful to me. As I went away to college, we exchanged cassette tapes. It was important to me that she hear the sounds of life where I was and not just me talking. I also shared some of my music with her.

SPANISH

In 1989, I enrolled in JTPA again and was placed back at the Commission. I was not happy, but once again I decided to make it a positive experience. I began to network with the regional staff, and I was encouraged to coordinate a teen support group. A regional counselor began taking me to watch beep baseball games where I could meet blind adults.

Many of the clients of the Commission for the Blind spoke only Spanish. The bits of Spanish that I learned in order to communicate with children were not going to help me take messages when the Spanish-speaking counselor was out of the office. I thought of a plan, and we both thought it was perfect. I wrote down some key phrases that I could use to ask for a caller's name (with spelling), number, address, etc.

One problem arose. I was good enough at pronouncing Spanish that the callers thought I was a native speaker. So, they began telling me their stories, and I had to stop them and explain that I really didn't speak Spanish, and the counselor would call them back.

I coordinated outings, sent out a newsletter, and even planned a "camp-in" with blind adult mentors. Many teens who lived in inner-city Houston were hesitant or unable to come to events because of lack of transportation, shame about recent sight loss, or parental feelings about blindness. In some families, cultural attitudes about blindness made parents very hesitant to permit teens to even speak with me by phone. Girls spoke to me if parents were not home but hung up quickly if another family member arrived home. If I called and a parent answered, I simply gave my name and did not mention that I was affiliated with the Commission for the Blind.

I felt great pride when a couple of teens came to the camp-in who had never come to an event before. One boy and I had been speaking for several months. I knew that he had some sight, and I thought nothing of it. Most of the teenagers had more sight than I did.

But when Jorge and I met, he exclaimed, "Oh my God! You're white!"

"So what?" I said.

"I thought you were Spanish!" he said.

I realized then that like the parent callers, he had been deceived by my ability to speak whatever language the other person spoke. I had not done it on purpose to deceive him or mock him, and I felt deeply sorry. After a few minutes he realized this, and we continued to relate to each other as friends. But the first meeting had been very awkward.

ADA AND CRUSHED HOPE

During 1989 and 1990, I attended some events for families of young children so that I could serve as a mentor. As I held tiny babies who were newly diagnosed, I came to terms with my own feelings about blindness and society. I wanted life to be different for them than it had been for me. I wanted them to have the freedom to choose where they worked. I wanted them to be able to access their books.

The Americans with Disabilities Act was passed during the summer after I graduated from high school. It was both an excitement and a terror for me. I took American government during my senior year of high school; and I was aware that sometimes legislation did not always bring about the desired results. But I could not make this knowledge transfer to my understanding of the ADA. Two things were significant during the summer of 1990 that coincided with the passage of the ADA.

I enrolled in JTPA for a third year. Once again, I was placed at the Commission for the Blind. I decided this time that I needed diverse work experience. I disenrolled from JTPA and asked my mother about how I could volunteer at the hospital where she worked. She helped me to get in touch with someone to register as a volunteer, and shortly I was sent to talk with the nurses in the occupational therapy program about volunteering to assist patients with their exercises.

I liked this idea very much, and it should have worked. I had done nursing home visitation with a group from my church for a couple of years, and I was quite comfortable with older people. The patients were not the problem. Nor was the work itself.

I got to work and gently guided an 80-year-old lady who had had a stroke through exercises that would help her to restore the use of her right arm. I learned her exercise routine quickly and was able to recognize when she was completing it successfully.

The problem was that the staff were afraid of my cane. They didn't want me to use it. "There's stuff in the hall," the director said. "We don't have time to guide you.

Rage boiled up within me. I felt that I had been lied to during all the years when I had practiced using my cane with the orientation and mobility instructor. Every time I had expressed feelings of embarrassment or discussed incidents of bullying, the instructor had said, "It's like a third arm. When you use this, people will know you're safe."

Clearly, they didn't know. Now it was just as if I didn't even have a cane, except the cane made things a thousand times worse by crashing against carts in the hall and announcing, "Hel-looooo! Blind person coming!"

I explained that the cane was there to give me information and help me to stay safe.

My explanation wasn't good enough. The director didn't want me on the occupational therapy unit.

I next went to another unit and spoke to nurses about coming to read to patients. The nurse only wanted me for an hour a day. My family didn't want to drive for so few volunteer hours.

I quit my volunteer job without having done much work at all. I felt devastated and wondered how things would get any better.

At least I was at home during my last summer before college. I had a few last opportunities to go out with the teenagers from the Texas Commission for the Blind. Our best outing was a trip to Astro World which included a great Christian concert.

LEARNING TO CARE FOR MYSELF

With or without work, I had plenty to do that summer. I had not learned some of the vital life skills that are normal for children to learn in preparation for life away from home, such as how to eat socially, do one's own laundry and cook basic food items. I refused to go away to a rehabilitation center. I wanted to spend my summer relaxing, and I was more than a bit embarrassed about the fact that I was learning things my sister had been doing since she was ten years old. How humiliating to be coached on the proper way to hold eating utensils and cut meat at the age of 18! I would almost rather have hidden in a hole than done this.

I didn't want strangers teaching me. I had never told my parents about the girls cursing at me at the school for the blind after I found them making fun of me. I certainly did not want a repeat of that experience. But I remembered it every time I tried to work on new skills. Who was thinking these things about me everywhere I went?

I knew that I needed to learn the skills, but I lashed out emotionally at authority figures who tried to teach me. If learning new skills was going to be so stressful, I wanted to do it in the comfort of my own home and from people who could allow me to feel my distress and wouldn't laugh at the silly reward system I devised to motivate myself to learn.

My mother and I set up a notebook with a listing of all the skills I was trying to remember to use each day. At a teachers' supply store, we bought packages of gold star stickers. Each day my mom stuck on various numbers of stickers beside each skill indicating how I was doing so that I could evaluate my progress in private. If I needed improvement, I could ask my questions when I was emotionally ready for feedback.

I did not find learning stressful when it occurred informally or when my teacher was a friend. Becky, a friend from the old days of Mrs. Richards Class who was several years older, patiently answered my questions about her techniques, encouraging me to try new skills and letting me know that she had experienced the same frustrations.

From Becky, I learned that the stove would not zap me if I allowed myself the freedom to experiment with cooking and cleaning methods. By doing this I was able to discover what worked for me and discard what did not. As I gained more experience, I experimented with new recipes as well. I loved to bake, and I became fairly good at preparing different types of cookies, brownies and bars. In time, I even started inventing my own recipes.

Over time, I also learned to communicate with my parents about my needs and to set up times when teaching would take place so that I could prepare myself emotionally. I also developed ways to help them understand how I learned and what information was most helpful to me. My dad was quite adept at discovering things he could point out to me, such as the change of the texture of scrambled eggs and ground beef as they cooked.

LONG-DISTANCE MENTOR

During my teen years, I began exchanging recorded letters on cassette tape with a friend of a family member named Shelva Jean Pickler. She was a retired schoolteacher who had lost her sight in the 1970s due to a neurological condition. My family member thought that we might be able to encourage each other. I was young and learned all my skills eagerly. Shelva Jean was vibrantly positive, and I suspect that my family member thought that she might be able to speak encouragement to the deep depression that I was struggling with as a young teenager.

My family member was right. Shelva Jean knew just the right things to say. Recorded letters did not arrive quickly in those days, but often they arrived at a time when I needed a bit of encouragement. I always recognized Shelva Jean's letters because they arrived in a little box with mailing labels on the flaps. When I wanted to mail my tape to her, all I needed to do was reverse the flaps and stick it in the mailbox.

One evening shortly after I quit my volunteer job, Shelva Jean called me. It was the first time we ever spoke by phone. I was thrilled to hear from her! It was also another instance of perfect timing. I poured out my heart, and she poured encouragement into me.

I lost touch with Shelva Jean sometime in the 1990s, but I absorbed some of the lessons she taught me. I also wanted to give to others what she had given to me.

16

ANDERSON

Finally, the big day came for my move to Anderson. My parents packed the car full of boxes and suitcases, and we all headed for Anderson. The dorms were not open yet, so we stayed with my great-grandmother.

By the time in my life that I am writing these memories down, there are many things that run together, some of which seem as if they should be related but can no longer be neatly fit. It seems there was some time that I stayed alone at my great-grandmother's house; but I cannot match this with the fact that my parents moved me into the dorm and helped me learn my way around campus during that first year. I do remember a few things that stood out about being at my great-grandmother's house.

My great-grandmother was not used to being around anyone who was blind. She placed a call to my uncle and asked, "What if she gets the shower too hot?"

He said, "I guess she'll turn it down."

"What if she falls down!"

"I guess she'll get up."

I'm not sure whether she ever got over her terror over the disasters that could befall me, but I had a good time hearing her stories. I also had a good time finding some new ways to terrorize her.

She believed firmly that cats belonged outside—and they should be as far from her property as possible. She owned a BB gun and used it to shoot cats that wandered onto her property. I enjoyed her exclamation of great disbelief when I told her about my current sleeping partner, Casey.

"A cat sleeps in your bed with you?" she howled. "Oh my!"

GETTING AROUND

I seem to remember Mom and Dad staying a day or two after I moved into the dorm, but I don't really know how long they were there. There are many small things I remember. Mom sewed pink hearts onto my pillowcases and towels so that I would be able to identify them by touch. No one else had a pink heart like my mom's. I remember her going down to the basement with me to be sure that I could work the laundry machines. In those days the laundry machines had dials that I could turn and memorize. Today I often hear stories of great frustration regarding laundry machines and accessibility.

I often hear people advise parents to request first-floor rooms for blind college students because it will make fire drills easier. I don't remember the fire drills. I remember schlepping my laundry to the basement and going to the basement for tornado drills. I don't suppose, after so much basement visitation, that the first-floor room made that much difference to me.

During the time while my parents were still there, Dad gave me a crash course in getting around on campus. He enlarged a campus map on a poster board and traced all of the sidewalks and buildings with puffy paint. We walked to and from various buildings over and over until I began to feel comfortable. I carried the map with me during the first few weeks as I learned my way around campus, first with Dad's help and then on my own.

Since my parents had not walked around with me much when I used my cane, being together on the AU campus brought new opportunities for us to learn how to interact. It never occurred to me that I would have to teach my parents about the cane until one day when we were leaving my dorm for one of our excursions with the map.

The path out of the dorm went down a terrace that had a long sidewalk with several pairs of short and long steps. As I came to the first step down, my mom stuck her arm out in front of me, to prevent me from falling. My cane came in contact with the drop-off at the same time that I stumbled over my mom's arm.

I became angry at my mom for stopping me. "You can't do that!" I shouted. You're not letting me figure out what the cane is telling me."

"I don't want you to get hurt," she said.

"I have to do this," I said. "That's why I spent all the time with Mr. Reed. If you don't let me go, then it doesn't matter."

"I'm just scared."

"Fine, but you have to let me do it anyway, like roller-skating."

After some time, I no longer needed the map. However, it attracted a good deal of attention from other students who were curious to know how I could learn from a map and who wanted to touch it.

There was one disadvantage of my use of the map. I was not well acquainted with the general layout of the campus. If something was not on the map, it did not exist in my mind. If I could not figure out how to connect a bunch of winding sidewalks and I got lost, I stopped exploring a particular area. As a result, I stuck to familiar routes when I was alone. The middle of the campus, known as "the valley," was made up of many winding and intersecting sidewalks which connect the library and other frequently used buildings. I never traveled through this area alone as an undergraduate student. I feared it.

MY SEARCH FOR FRIENDS

Screen reading technology was in its infancy at this time. While I had used some early-model note-taking devices in high school, I became terrified when my dad told me that he was going to buy me a computer for college. My fear had no impact on him. He bought it; and he made me learn to use it. In those days, computers were not operated with graphical interface and mouse. Each command was typed in deliberately. If I wanted to write a paper, I typed "open wp" to open WordPerfect.

I brought my desktop computer, which was equipped with standard word processing software and a screen-reading program which read text from the screen aloud in synthetic speech. The speech was so poor that it sounded like a drunk person with a mouth full of cotton. Still, it was a novelty, and it drew a great amount of attention.

In class, I wrote notes in braille on a handheld device called a slate and stylus—literally punching one dot at a time. In the evenings, I studied using books on cassette. Because my memory was so poor, I punched out notes while reading my books on tape as well.

People were very curious about how I accomplished my work, about how my computer functioned, etc. I hoped that their curiosity might give way to friendship in time. This progression didn't often take place. The more I fielded questions about blindness that did not progress toward authentic social encounters, the more depressed I became. The problem came to a head one afternoon.

I put up signs around campus to solicit readers since most of my textbooks were not available in recorded format. Some of the people who responded seemed very nice; and I would have liked to know them as friends. I got into the habit of leaving the text and a cassette tape with them so that they could bring it back and we would not have to deal with the hassle of trying to coordinate our schedules for reading and studying time. This way, I would also have the material to refer back to later.

When my reader came to pick up material for my English class, I warmed up to her immediately. She was soft-spoken and friendly. "If you ever need anything, call me," she said as she took the book and tape. How sweet, I thought. Then she said the words I hated to hear. "It must be such a challenge for you to be here!"

I was sure that she hadn't meant anything uncomplimentary by it; but as she left, I felt dejected. Would I ever make a real friend? Or would everyone think that I lived in a world of "challenge?" I could not bear the weight of the pain I felt. Something needed to change.

On that day, I practiced advocacy for the first time. I requested my reader's friendship, explaining in a letter that socialization, not blindness, was my challenge. Sending the letter was terrifying; but not sending it meant giving in to the negative emotions.

My letter resulted in the formation of one friendship. My friend often took me to Miller Chapel, which was across the valley from my dorm, where we shared times of prayer late in the evening. Our friendship continued through the first semester of my freshman year. She graduated in December, and we wrote occasional letters after that time.

A DARK PLACE

I attempted to maintain a lighthearted attitude about using the cane at AU. However, my lighthearted attitude collapsed when I tripped someone. I dubbed my cane "the ankle slapper" in order to cope with my embarrassment and continued to walk to class independently much of the time.

I still couldn't move my wrist quickly enough to run or even to walk briskly with the cane; and I had to stop a conversation in order to figure out what my cane was touching or pull it out of sidewalk cracks.

I also experienced difficulties hearing when people who were walking ahead of me called back to give me directions. This made it very difficult for me to walk with someone. When I wanted to hold a conversation while walking, I chose to walk holding on to the arm of my companion—using "sighted guide."

Unfortunately, my use of sighted guide became a thorn in my flesh. People at the college began to assume that I was dependent on my companions and even to refer to me as self-centered. When I was seeking a roommate for the spring semester of my freshman year, one girl responded, "I can't escort you everywhere like you want."

As my depression deepened during that first year, I began to have thoughts of self-harm. I sought assistance from a counselor. My counseling sessions were comforting; but the counselor was unable to identify the source of the problems. She stated that I seemed bright and well-adjusted.

I had heard these things before, when I saw the counselor following the mysterious symptoms during my high school years. There seemed to be a discrepancy between the counselor's perception, which matched my understanding of myself, and my peers' perception of me. What was the reason for this discrepancy?

Unable to resolve the question, I chose to attempt to accommodate what I perceived to be the needs and wishes of my peers. Since they perceived that I was dependent on them to "escort me" from here to there, I minimized the "need" for them to do so. I stopped walking to class with a group of nice girls who seemed friendly and had invited me to join them; and I stopped eating in the cafeteria. This increased my loneliness; but I reasoned that my loneliness did not matter.

In the spring of my freshman year, I moved into a private room. I longed for the companionship which I perceived other students had with their roommates. During this time God blessed me with a friend, Angi. She and her boyfriend faithfully included me in many activities, ate with me in the cafeteria, and encouraged me and prayed with me when I felt most alone. I experienced tremendous anxiety concerning my suitability as a friend, especially since Angi and Greg were dating. Perhaps they would become tired of including me as a tag-along at some point.

My social problems reached a climax that affected my spiritual life one evening during the spring of my freshman year while I was talking to some girls in a dorm room. One of the girls suddenly decided to take a walk to a nearby Christian bookstore and asked if anyone would like to go with her.

"I'd like to go," I said. I thought that it would be fun to walk together, continue talking, and visit the Christian bookstore all in one outing.

"Oh," she said dismissively, "I have a meeting, and I have to be back in a hurry. But would anyone else like to go?"

There was a hush in the room. Everyone knew what the truth was. There was no meeting, but I was not invited.

I left the room as the rest of the girls were reluctantly refusing to go. It was awkward for everyone. The girls were her friends, but admitting they wanted to go would be equivalent to participating in what she was doing to me. I felt that my very presence put them in an awkward situation.

In my room, I wrestled with my understanding of theology. Was their behavior toward me sinful? If so, what did it mean for my relationship with Jesus? I had always thought of Jesus as my friend, a comforter when I was lonely. But Jesus was the friend of sinners, the one who died for sinners. What would he have done with me? Could Jesus be the friend of sinners and the friend of people who were hurt by sin at the same time?

I thought about Jesus, praying in the garden at Gethsemane, asking God to remove the cup from him. I imagined Jesus, thinking about sin. I thought that in order to think about sin, Jesus would also have thought about the harm that sin caused. Surely it would have hurt Jesus to think of people harming each other.

If nothing else, I thought, I could still know Jesus as comforter. While he was praying those agonizing prayers alone in the garden, his companions fell asleep. Jesus knew loneliness better than anyone else.

17

THE GRAY
CURTAIN—AGAIN

Impromptu theological discussions were not uncommon at Anderson University. Often these discussions were encouraging emotionally and helped me to expand my understanding of a concept. Occasionally, however, they were deeply disturbing.

Beginning my studies at Anderson University was a new cultural experience for me. I had grown up attending public schools; and though I had attended church several times a week and was quite eager for deep study of the Bible and application of its concepts to my life, I was unprepared for the excessive use of church lingo that surrounded me. Everyday conversations were filled with phrases like "God's will," "calling," "a word from the Lord," etc. I found that often portions of the Bible were quoted out of context. Still, I hoped that as we all matured, we would learn to use wisdom as we practiced our faith. We often held theological discussions in various dorm rooms; and these sometimes assisted in clarifying our understanding of theological concepts and passages of Scripture.

THE CONFRONTATION

One night in February 1991, as a group of girls were holding a discussion in my room, the conversation turned to the topic of healing. Several girls shared their understandings of the topic. At last, a girl stated that she believed that healing was an experience which naturally followed salvation.

I felt my face redden with anger. The implication of her statement was that if I was really saved, I would have been healed of my blindness! Who was she to judge me, and where had God promised this? If she was right, then what was wrong with me? I was a good girl. I prayed often—even several times a day. I didn't always read my Bible, but I tried to apply what I read. I didn't say hurtful things. I never questioned whether Jesus died to save me. But I was blind and not healed!

Desperate for understanding, I challenged her statement. "Maybe God doesn't always heal," I said. "I was born early, and I'm alive. That's the miracle He gave when my parents prayed."

"Are you sure your parents didn't just say, 'As long as You let her live?'" she asked.

Anger erupted inside me. My parents' instruction was the foundation of my faith. How could she tear that foundation down by questioning their faith? She didn't even know them!

I was deeply troubled. What if all that my parents had taught me was wrong? What if I was not really a Christian? What if my parents had never really prayed with faith for my healing?

The girls left my room late that night. I tried to let the discussion go—I had an early class the next morning. But sleep eluded me. I needed to talk to someone about this—someone much wiser than I.

In fact, I needed to talk to more than one someone. The foundation of my faith was shaken, and I no longer knew whose opinion to trust. I consulted my pastor, my uncle, and some of my professors. I even started reading the Bible excessively, searching desperately for the truth about healing. After a few weeks, I summoned my courage to ask God to heal me. I became convinced that I had heard a promise in my mind, and I began to believe that He would heal me in time.

QUESTIONS

I tried to believe that healing could come at any time, but I struggled with feelings of disappointment and doubt. In July 1991, I discovered the passage in the ninth chapter of John where Jesus tells the disciples that the reason that a man was born blind was so that the work of God could be displayed in him. I knew that Jesus had then healed the man, but I tried to content myself with the idea that the work of God did not have to be healing. It could be anything that brought other people into His Kingdom.

I buoyed myself with this idea and planned a concert at my church for August 1991. After all, I had something perfectly useful for building the Kingdom: music.

More people attended the concert than I could have expected! Standing in the lobby afterward, I became misty as people greeted me and told me deeply personal stories about what the music meant to them. It was a night I would cherish forever, though I did not know the reason for many more months.

CHANGES

During the summer of 1991, I traveled to Morristown, New Jersey, to attend four weeks of training with a Seeing Eye dog. The trip was a long-anticipated one but also provoked numerous anxieties. Whether bringing a dog guide into my life would improve my situation at AU or not was something only time would tell.

I first saw a dog guide at work when I was sixteen years old.

I became acquainted with a rehabilitation counselor who had a dog guide. She encouraged me to pet the dog and examine her harness. I had always been rather afraid of dogs; and I was impressed with this dog, who lay quietly on the floor and did not jump on me or lick my face. At that moment, I knew that I wanted a dog like that.

I learned later that dog guides do not always follow the rules about no jumping and no licking. They only follow the rules if I make and keep them. Elli, the strong, stocky black Labrador retriever who became my guide, seemed to know intuitively how much I hated to be licked; but she had boundless energy and a loud bark and used them often. I eventually learned to correct her for barking at noises she heard in the dorm hallway.

At AU, students had mixed reactions to Elli. Some were intrigued by her. Others wanted nothing to do with her. One day as I was taking an afternoon nap, I heard a student complain as she walked down the hall, "It smells like dawg!" I wondered irritably whether she was as offended by the smells of people's garbage as she was by the faint dog scent that could not ever be completely eliminated by good grooming.

THE GRAY CURTAIN RETURNS

Difficulties with social relationships were not the only troubles that visited me at AU. An equally disturbing trouble was the return of the gray curtain. Its return was different this time. It wasn't related to neurological symptoms; and it would send me into a battle for my remaining vision that would last for many years.

Early on the morning of October 4, 1991, I put the harness on Elli and set out for class. It was a chilly morning in Indiana, and I looked forward to getting the walk across campus over, even if it was a short walk. I headed out the side door of Myers Hall and down the sidewalk that led between Myers and Morrison Hall, where most of the freshman girls lived. Once I reached the front of the buildings, I would turn right and head for the main walk in front of Morrison, leading to the street where I would cross over to the main part of campus.

But something was wrong. The pavement under my feet was not concrete. It was asphalt. Where was I? I must be in the parking lot! I must be between two cars. But I should be able to see over the tops of them. Why couldn't I see over the tops? Why couldn't I see the sky? It wasn't sunny, but it wasn't dark either.

The gray curtain had returned—and this time it did not go away in a few hours. Not only this, but I was not on a small familiar campus like TSB, where I could pick my way along a sidewalk and find my house. I could not go home and lie down. I needed to go to class; and going to class meant getting out of wherever I was, going across streets and parking lots and through sidewalk mazes.

Did I trust Elli enough to do this? Upon finding out that I was getting a Seeing Eye dog, my aunt asked me if I could just give her a building name and expect her to go there. The answer was no. It was my responsibility to give the directions. I couldn't do it in the dark!

I tried anyway. "Elli, forward," I said through blubbery tears.

She went. I could not feel the road under my feet. My body shook. But we arrived. I stuffed myself into my chair. And the professor started to speak. I usually liked his class. He was the campus pastor, and he had a nice, soothing voice.

TERROR IN CLASS

"Why should we believe in God?" the professor asked.

What is he doing? I wondered.

He began to tell a story about a former student who came to his office once to tell him that her father had been killed by a drunk driver. "I don't know if I believe in God anymore," she said.

He finished his story and repeated his question. "Why should we believe in God?"

I wanted to un-stuff myself from my desk and run away from the room. But I did not want to make a scene. Why indeed. I never asked God to heal me. I didn't need a miracle. I just trusted Him to take care of me, not to betray me. Wasn't it enough that

I was bullied, that I was undesirable as a friend because I was blind? Did He have to make it worse?

STIRRING THOUGHTS

In November, I attended a conference in Indianapolis called Praise Gathering. The conference lasted the entire weekend, and I attended several seminars given by different speakers. Sheila Walsh spoke about receiving a letter from a woman who had leukemia. In the letter, the woman asked, "Why do you always talk about healing? Why don't you talk about the people who are blind who are serving God...?"

I spent the rest of the time in the seminar weeping. While I wanted to be healed, I also felt the reality of the words in that letter. I was blind and I was serving God, and I wanted to be part of the body of Christ. But it seemed that I couldn't be unless I was healed.

A PRAYER FOR HEALING

During the fall months of 1991, when the sun rarely shown in Indiana, I forgot about the gray curtain. My memory of how the world was supposed to appear took over. In my mind I saw all of the buildings looming around me, the contrast between sidewalk and grass, the outlines of cars, the sharp contrast between the snow and Elli. However, when I returned home to Texas, the sun was shining brightly through the windows—it must be since I could feel its warmth—but I could not see the furniture in the house or the dark shape of Elli sitting on the patio waiting to come into the house. Panicked, I saw the ophthalmologist. It was then that I was diagnosed with glaucoma. The doctor did not know whether treatment would bring about improvement in my vision.

On January 23, 1992, I decided to tell God once and for all how I felt. I had been attempting to read through the New Testament, but it seemed that every time I began reading, I was reading about people who had been healed. By this day, I had finally had enough. Was healing available today or not? If not, then I didn't want to read about it. If so, then I didn't want to believe in a God who obviously didn't think I was good enough to deserve it. I threw down my braille Bible and started typing in my journal on my computer. I unleashed all the desires I had hidden for the previous six months while trying to convince myself that God would use me as I was and that the desire for healing was a stumbling block placed in the way of my spiritual growth by Satan. I released all the pain which had been building since my visit to the doctor.

> *The desire won't leave me, Lord. I don't know why.... I don't want to focus on it—I have been over this and over it and over it before; what else can I say? But I have to ask You for it....*

A MIRACLE?

Immediately after writing those words, I lifted up my head—and gasped. How could my mind play such evil tricks on me?

Or had my roommate really left the reading light on over her desk? I crossed the room and held my hand under the lamp. It was warm.

Unsure whether to be excited or confused, I called Angi at the campus box office, where she was working for the afternoon. "I don't know what to think of this," I told her.

After I finished the story, Angi suggested that I accompany her to a Bible study led by the pastor of her small charismatic church. Although I was not entirely comfortable with a charismatic church, I agreed to go, thinking that perhaps I could gain some understanding of what was happening to me.

We arrived at the pastor's home after dark. I approached the house hesitantly. As I neared the door, I saw a light in the window. Just like the lights in the hallway at the hospital, that lamp showed me that I was not dreaming. God had answered my doubt by building my faith.

THE CURTAIN PULLED BACK

There was no medical explanation for the improvement I began to experience on January 23, 1992. Over the next few days, my vision continued to improve. By January 26, it was once again useful for locating doorways and large objects which could serve as landmarks.

Over the next few months, I experienced periods of extreme light sensitivity which were followed by clearing of my vision. After each of these periods I would notice that there were a few minor improvements in what I could see. One evening in April,

I identified the color pink, something which I had not done since childhood.

In May 1992, I saw the doctor again. Despite the improvements in my vision, my pressure remained dangerously high. I was referred to a glaucoma specialist in Houston who confirmed this fact. "You need to have surgery as soon as possible," he stated emphatically.

Shocked, I questioned him. "But my vision is fine," I protested.

"With your pressure at this level," he acknowledged gravely, "you could lose that vision at any time."

The surgery was done one week later, on June 8. I was given no hope of improvement in my vision.

My vision improved. The doctor could not explain the improvement; but it was my experience. I was given drops to put in my eyes to keep the pressure down and told that I would probably need them for the rest of my life.

What I wish had never happened during that time were the prophecies. Sighted people got very excited upon hearing about the improvements and began to pray and prophesy over me, saying that I would see by a certain time. I did not. I wonder today whether God spoke to them or whether they were so eager for me to experience a miracle of full healing that they imagined a date, like the men who prophesy that the Rapture is coming when no man knows the day or the hour. I was young and had no experience or teaching in how to interpret a true from a false prophecy or how to test the spirits; and I trusted every word that came from the mouth of a person who said they were a Christian. This left me open to a great deal of personal and spiritual woundedness.

MY DECISION

During the second semester of my sophomore year, Angi and I shared a room. She and Greg established Friday night as their date night and included me in activities on other nights. I learned to cope with their absence and to look forward to activities in which I was included.

Elli's work made it easier for me to get where I needed to go quickly on campus. However, my general social situation continued to deteriorate, and my depression continued to mount. In the spring of 1992, in one of my ministry classes, a classmate spoke up one day and asked the group why people rolled their eyes when I contributed something to the discussion. I appreciated her support, but it was late in the game. I felt that wherever I went, eyes rolled.

Worn down and defeated, I made a decision to transfer out of Anderson University. I knew that I was running away and giving up what I loved. I could not major in Christian ministries or music business at a state university. But I had other interests. Surely, I could find a way to be happy in another career. The state university was big. Perhaps I would make friends there.

I spoke only to my parents about my decision to transfer. My parents were concerned about my mental health and my difficulty in forming friendships. They thought that I might have more social opportunities at a bigger campus. If I had spoken to a pastor, perhaps the person would have told me something important that I needed to know before I made my choice. When you leave one place, you take all of the pain from the old place with you, and you then have to deal with it without any of the supports you had in the old place, small and frail though they might be.

By transferring, I lost access to my pastors, my existing counselors, and my friendships with Angi and Greg. I also had to begin a new educational journey from the start. While doing this, I had to cope with several sources of deep emotional and spiritual pain that developed at the end of my second year at AU.

18

"ALWAYS STAY WITH GOD"

When I began my studies at AU in the fall of 1990, I felt great excitement about studying music business. My courseload during the first semester was to include music theory — or so I thought. I had a very positive attitude about this, expecting that it would help to strengthen my songwriting ability.

There was a problem. The dean of the music department felt that since I could not read print music, I should not take the course. He also did not tell me this. He told another professor who was a friend of a family member. She called my family member, who called my mother, who called me. The dean would permit me to take a non-credit music fundamentals course but otherwise he recommended that I take math.

It was a laughable recommendation. I was quite skilled in math, but my performance in geometry was everything he feared about music theory.

Being disallowed from taking music theory courses meant

that I would not be able to major in music business as I planned. I was devastated.

That evening, Granny called to ask how I was adjusting to life on campus. I started to cry and told her about the music disappointment.

"Don't they remember Dr. Hartselle?" she exclaimed.

"Who's Dr. Hartselle?" I asked. Inwardly, I wondered why Dr. Hartselle had anything to do with my problems.

"He was my piano teacher," she said. "He was the first piano teacher there, and he was blind."

I wasn't quite sure how to confront anyone about this informational jewel. The music problem at AU was worse than the Chorale problem. I didn't have the opportunity to go to the dean's office and confront him. He had run around me and gone through a number of people to give me the message that I wasn't welcome as if I couldn't cope with the news myself.

I would need to be creative, perhaps to run around the dean himself. "Why don't you ask Gloria Gaither to listen to one of your songs?" Granny asked.

"Oh, she wouldn't," I said. "Everybody wants her to listen to their songs."

"But you're a college student. Doesn't she teach a class there? Maybe you could take it."

"You have to take music theory first," I huffed.

"Maybe if you tell her what happened she would let you take it anyway, especially if she hears your music." My grandmother's soft, encouraging tone never wavered. She didn't get angry with my bad attitude or tell me to think positively. She just continued on with her confident belief that things would right themselves.

NOT GIVING UP

I had no confidence that Gloria would listen to me. But other people did. I became acquainted with some girls who were music majors, and they were also confident when I told them about my predicament. "Just call her," they said. "She will recognize you from the Sunday school class at church. She's one of the teachers for the college students. She'll probably listen to you play after class."

They were right. I gathered my courage and called one evening, introducing myself as a student in her Sunday school class. She recognized me right away and asked how I was doing? I launched into my story and told her how the decision had impacted me. Finally, I said, "Would you listen to one of my songs and maybe think about letting me take your class? If I could pass your class, they might let me take music theory."

On a Sunday morning in November 1990, my hands trembled as I played a brand-new song for her immediately following Sunday school. She said very little. I learned later that this did not indicate negative opinion. She gave me permission to take her class in the spring of 1991. In the class, I wrote a new song and also wrote a research paper about a topic related to songwriting. The paper was marked up so heavily that I could feel mark dents throughout every page. Beyond my comprehension, it was also given an A.

DOWNHILL

In the spring of 1991, my family learned that Granny's breast cancer had metastasized to the lungs. She was tired and no longer played Scrabble or went to church. She devoted her energy to a project we did not know about until later.

At Christmastime in 1991, our family had a large gathering where Granny was able to participate. In the spring of 1992, her health began to decline rapidly.

I returned to AU and attempted to carry on normally. My attempt failed miserably. I could not concentrate on my music theory class, and I didn't care about how to formulate room modes in my recording techniques class. All I cared about was being present for Granny, or perhaps actually doing some recording for her. I was scheduled to sing in chapel in April, and I did care about that. It was a rare opportunity, and I was deeply honored that I was chosen.

STRANGE FEELINGS

Late one night in February 1992, I sat bolt upright in bed and could not go back to sleep. I just sat still and felt expectant. Something was changing.

My phone rang. Who was calling so late at night? Angi stirred across the room in her bed, but she didn't seem bothered by the phone. Instead, she said, "Yeah, the Latin American empires are coming. It's just like last night but last night there were five hundred thousand of them and tonight there are only eighteen thousand."

My dad was on the phone. He gently told me that a bone scan showed that the cancer had spread throughout Granny's body and she likely had a few weeks left. He promised to pick me up when I came home for spring break and said that the family would be sure that I had some time with her.

During spring break, I brought homework and asked to borrow my parents' computer. We installed my screen reader and discovered that I could play Hangman. We all laughed when the screen reader mispronounced the words "Nice try. But no cigar!" which the game displayed to the loser. To me it read, "Nice try dot but no sigger bang."

My parents left me home alone while they went off to work, and I puttered around on their computer. While looking for the location where my files were stored, I found a file that was just called "Granny". I could not get over my curiosity. Did Granny write something? Would she be mad if I read it?

I opened the file and read: "...I hope that one day my children will read this...."

Surely, she also would want her grandchildren to read. I kept reading. And Reading. She wrote about her memories of growing up in rural Nebraska, and serving as the church secretary, and teaching Sunday school.

We all kept trying not to cry in front of Granny. The most frequent question asked of her was, "Do you want to go to bed?" Meanwhile she worried about how we were doing.

Finally, one evening, Mom and I emerged from a private crying session in the back bedroom only to find someone else crying in the front room, which had been converted into a specialized room for Granny. We all thought that Granny would be falling asleep soon since she had been given a sleeping pill. She was not sleeping, and she joined in the crying. Mom and I began to cry again, and we were all surprised at how relieved we felt to have the crying out in the open.

When we all dried our tears, someone got out a hymnal and started singing hymns. Granny still remembered all the words and did her best to sing along. I had some blank tapes in my purse, and I stuck one in Granny's recorder to capture a few memories. We ended up singing for a couple of hours, and Granny made some requests about her memorial service. She asked specifically that the pastor not sing.

"Why?" Mom asked, laughing.

"He sings too loud."

I returned to AU after spring break and found that I had been invited to sing in chapel just prior to Easter. But I could not concentrate on anything. I could not sleep at night. I felt as if I was still in Granny's room and something was deeply wrong.

Finally, I went and took a long, hot shower and tried to clear my mind, and I prayed. I only had enough money for one more plane ticket. I could not waste it. What did God want me to do?

My mind remained unclear. So, I called my aunt Cheryl. "What would you do?" I asked.

"Let me tell you what happened last night," she said. Granny's cancer was beginning to affect her brain and to cause her to experience distorted thinking, but she spoke of my partial healing and of her desire for other family members to believe in God.

My uncle Mike felt strongly that I would be aware if Granny

was distressed and urged me to trust my discernment. After a couple more days of emotional and spiritual distress, I bought the last ticket on a flight to Houston.

Visiting Granny was painful. She was in extreme pain and was not lucid. She did not recognize us and thought that we were going to hurt her. At home, I cried and asked my dad, "Why is God allowing this?"

Dad encouraged me to remember that "this isn't Granny." I understood, but that didn't explain to me why God allowed it.

Shortly afterward, Mom called to tell me that Granny was resting peacefully.

I took comfort in remembering our last conversation when I was alone with her during spring break. She said to me, "You have a gift from God," she said. "Always be faithful to Him. You can never go wrong when you trust Him."

I remained at home for another week. During that time, Granny experienced several moments of lucidity during the week. She was able to make a number of requests for prayer and for things that gave her comfort, such as foot massages and more family singing.

JUST DAYS AGO

When I returned to AU, the professor who arranged for me to sing in chapel greeted me with anger. "Why did you do this?"

I responded with my own anger. "Don't you remember what is happening in my family?"

"I was afraid you would not be back to do this!" She exclaimed.

"I have not forgotten, and I will sing." One of my strong commitments in life is that I always sing, even in deepest despair. I would have sung while this was happening, just as I sang on that night when the suicidal thoughts tormented me as a 15-year-old.

I would never have forgotten my commitment. I would have moved heaven and earth to be there. She had no way to know this. But this week she would learn it.

As I sat in chapel on April 6, waiting to sing, I agonized over the words I heard from the monotone voice of my computer that morning, reading my email to me. "Granny probably has three to six days left."

Yes, I would sing about Gethsemane. Then I would record the song I had recently written about the week I spent with Granny. I had no hope of being with her in her last days. But I could send her music. Perhaps it would be comforting to her.

Granny requested my music. And she held on. At one point several weeks earlier, she had made a joke, so we thought, about how amusing it would be to meet Jesus on Easter. It now appeared that she would have a chance.

HOLY THINGS

My mother bought me a ticket home on Easter weekend. Ten days had passed since I received that email. Granny was silent and her breathing was greatly labored and crackly. She was given Morphine frequently for pain and relaxation.

I went home from the hospital on Saturday night, April 18, with extreme reluctance. My mom and aunt Cheryl stayed overnight.

In the middle of the night, Elli got up and sat in my doorway like a guard dog instead of a guide dog. My dad came down the hall and asked if she was ok. I thought she was fine but had no idea why she was guarding.

My dad had just received a call from my mom, asking us to come immediately to the hospital. The nurses had told her that Granny's death was nearing.

We arrived shortly before 5:00 A.M. Granny's breathing had quieted. We all began to sing hymns, and I held Granny's hand. Mom told us that before we arrived, she said to Granny that it was Easter morning, and one tear fell from Granny's eye. At 5:05 on Easter morning, 1992, Granny's deep desire was realized.

There are many days when I wish that I had more time on earth with Granny. But I also treasure things she left behind for me that represent her legacy to me: her writings, recordings of her singing and her interactions with family, books that belonged to her, and especially the thought of what she would think of knowing that for seven years I lived in Dr. Hartselle's house.

I haven't always trusted God as she instructed me to do. I have experienced the consequences of failing to do so. Not the God-punishes-me consequences that people often preach about but the consequence of losing my own way and thus falling out of relationship with God. In falling out of relationship with God, it is I who find my own punishment, and I am the one who ascribes the motive of punishment to God. If Granny had been alive to talk to me about this, she would probably have used that same voice she used when I was huffing about the music department and said, "Just try talking to God again. He will listen."

19

VICKI

While I was training with Elli, I made friends with several people who were using an online service called GE-Nie. "We need to get you a modem so you can get online and stay in touch," one of them said.

This idea of using a computer to stay in touch was completely foreign to me. I loved getting my mail at AU and finding that someone had written me a braille letter: my very own mail that I could read! If I used a modem, I wouldn't be getting letters in braille. I felt a great letdown. But if my parents got one too, then we could write to each other, and my family's mail would be private! I would not get any more printed letters that I would need someone to read to me.

I didn't intend to use my modem for anything but emailing my friends from guide dog school and my family. But that was before I learned that my friends from guide dog school were doing something called playing on the BBS.

Today we are online everywhere. We don't need wires connected to our computers. We are charged one monthly rate for our Internet access. We can all talk to each other regardless of what service we use to connect. Our access interface options all offer us the same things: email and web pages, games to play, etc. Being online does not mean we can't talk on the phone.

In 1991, we had to connect our computers to the phone line in order to access our services. Users of AOL could not play games with users of CompuServe. Users of CompuServe could not participate on BBS systems (multi-user forums) with users of GE-Nie. There was no WWW accessible to all these services. For the most part, email was limited to users of the same service. We paid a low rate for access to the service between 6:00 P.M. and 8:00 A.M. During the day we paid a very high "prime time" rate. Additionally, if our access number was outside our local calling area, we also paid long-distance charges.

Each service had its own client (a kind of "app") that could be downloaded. The client made it possible for the user to connect, download all the data for the things one participated in, and then manage the data and compose responses offline, thus limiting paid time online. So, one could download email and all the posts to forums where one was subscribed, hang up, and read and respond offline, and reconnect to post the responses— and of course download more posts for reading later.

I learned soon that there was not only a disability forum but also a religion forum and a writers' forum—and many other forums. I dove deep into the online world. And I found places where people argued the merits of belief in a God who healed. Finding this forum in the fall of 1991, when I was wrestling with vision loss, was like stepping into a fire.

It was not only a fire for me. It was a place where I encountered the pain of others. Sometimes they were people who were just plain hostile, and I didn't know why. Sometimes they were people who identified as disabled. On this forum I met a gentle lady with amyotrophic lateral sclerosis (ALS). She never had an unkind word to say toward anyone, regardless of how unkind they were toward her. How I longed to be like her! But I had not yet developed gentleness nor patience in my soul.

I also met another lady, Vicki, on this forum. I thought our communications would stay there. But she had other ideas, like becoming my friend via email. She liked what I posted. *What in the world,* I thought? I was just writing things!

I supposed that if she really wanted to be actual friends, she ought to know the truth—you know, the truth about me being blind, so that she could have the option of going away like other people did at AU. So, I just told her: "You should know that I am blind."

I was just writing things, giving her choices. But she was not. Vicki's words were always intentional.

I didn't know on that day how to save email. I wish I had. Vicki's email back to me was the nicest thing I ever read. She wrote about how my blindness didn't matter, that my heart mattered and she could see it in what I wrote. She had intentions to take me under her wing and assist me on my journey of learning to pray and interact well online.

Things had a tendency to just fall out of me like water sometimes, and sometimes I really wished I could take them back later.

But she liked what I wrote and thought my heart showed in

my writing. Her email was something I treasured in my heart.
I soon learned how to save mail, and the vast majority of my
correspondence with Vicki is now a real treasure as well as a
heart treasure.

We carried on a deep and verbose correspondence. We learned
that we lived near one another. Eventually we met in person.
Our friendship took on a new character from that point forward.
We met as often as we could to bolster our online correspondence with "real-life" fellowship, but in truth our correspondence was the life of our fellowship.

Her marriage was quite unhappy, and my dog behaved in
a very protective manner toward her when her husband was
with us.

Vicki encouraged me to dig deep in my reading of Scripture,
to trust the Holy Spirit and deepen my understanding of what
discernment means, and to trust in God's power to heal even
when I didn't personally experience it.

She pointed me gently to discussions on the forum and gave
me guidance about how to conduct myself, sometimes talking
to me about background information and previous interactions
that I was too new to the forum to have known. Her background
information helped me to think about what I was reading as
something more than hateful words on a screen and to understand how it might come from a person who had been deeply
wounded and who might respond from pain instead of a desire
to play games and see how they could make a Christian squirm.

Vicki was very concerned about my depression episodes. She
felt that I expected too much of myself where my mental health

was concerned. She encouraged me to disclose my depression to my parents and request psychiatric treatment, even to take a year off school if necessary. It took several years before I took any time for myself.

In the summer of 1992, when I had surgery on my eye, Vicki was resting after psychiatric treatment. She and her husband were going through intensive counseling, hoping to repair difficulties in their marriage. But in late June, Vicki called me and spoke very quietly.

Her husband had become violent and had started drinking again, and she was planning to leave. She disconnected at 8:00 A.M., prime time.

I had a near-uncontrollable urge to call her back. I ignored it. It was too expensive.

That was the last time I spoke to her. Days later, her husband called me and calmly informed me that "Vicki died."

I asked what happened.

"She just died." He dissolved into tears.

Women who are 37 years old don't "just die." My heart felt that it would leap out of my chest. I did not want to talk to anyone or be with anyone. I thought that I should tell my parents that I needed to be alone, and they would probably want to know why.

I walked into their room. "Are you ok?" my dad asked.

A great guttural scream came from deep within me, and I could not make it stop.

"Vicki DIIIIIIED!" I wailed.

Vicki's husband called several times over the next few weeks.

Once he wanted to describe her memorial service: a service which I would have liked to attend. Once he wanted to yell at me and remind me that she loved him and always returned to him. Once he wanted to cry and ask why she died. I wouldn't know. I was only 20 years old.

Her death was ruled a suicide by police. Her husband may have had a history of violence, but her body had an extreme amount of medication in it.

I could not reconcile this with the person I knew. The person I knew made the effort of Job to cope with her pain. God was her rock and her fortress, and her faith was a model to me in my own distress. Her suicide was a genuine distress to me.

Years passed before I made peace with Vicki's death. Several of our other mutual friends seemed to have more ability to lay Vicki at the feet of Jesus than I had. Eventually I lost touch with everyone.

I wanted to know why God could let her die, why God didn't make her leave her husband sooner. I wanted to know whether she was with the God she loved so much or whether God rejected her because of her sin.

I finally came to the conclusion that if God was truly God (and surely He was), God was faithful to her broken heart in her most painful hour. God could decide on whom to show mercy as God wished. My insistence on knowing all the answers was clinging to the knowledge of things that belonged to God. I finally laid Vicki in the arms of Jesus her Savior.

Vicki and Granny were my best mentors in my journey of learning to trust the Holy Spirit and to exercise discernment.

Because their deaths were so close and my grief was so raw, I was not equipped for the things that lay ahead when I transferred to SFA in the fall of 1992, taking with me the struggle with my beliefs about healing and my unresolved griefs.

20

NEW SCHOOL, NEW EXPERIENCES

In the summer of 1992, my sight stabilized at the level where it had previously been. I began to forget about the gray curtain. That fall, when I transferred to Stephen F. Austin State University, I changed my major to education of the visually impaired.

Getting around the SFA campus was terrifying at first. I lived in a dorm which was located across a busy street from the main part of campus. In order to get to class, I had to locate a crosswalk and wait until there was no traffic—or until cars were gracious enough to stop for me. I was grateful to have a dog guide with me on the long walks to class. I often needed to cross parking lots and other areas with open space which would have intimidated me when using a cane.

Most of my sixty-six hours transferred; but they were counted as electives. So, I needed to take all of the basic courses over again as if beginning for the first time. This was annoying, but it was just a minor inconvenience that meant I would be in school for a long time. I worked hard and made it through "the basics"—sometimes with much better grades than others. I was still not good at learning from recorded materials, so I spent countless hours taking notes in braille from my cassette tapes.

In the fall of 1993, I enrolled in a class on the anatomy of the eye, a required course for teachers of the visually impaired. The course was taught by a local optometrist. I enjoyed his teaching style, and I was fascinated to learn about the parts of the eye and how they worked together.

I decided to ask the optometrist if he would evaluate me for glasses or contact lenses.

He agreed, and in the summer of 1994, I began wearing a custom-made contact lens with a high power. The lens was designed to fit my eye, which was smaller than the average person's eye. Once again, the world opened up to me. I could see objects more clearly and judge distances more accurately.

During 1994 and 1995, my pressure was relatively stable. I faithfully administered the eye drops prescribed for me in 1992. However, as people with glaucoma often do, I became too confident that my pressure was stable. I stopped using the medication—and I did not tell the optometrist. He began to express increasing concern and to urge me to see a glaucoma specialist. I ignored his advice—until April 1998. I was too busy with other aspects of my life, I reasoned, to worry about things like more eye exams. I wasn't losing vision, and my eyes felt fine.

NEW CROWD

The change of major meant that I was acquainted with new people who did not necessarily share my beliefs or behaviors. I began to go out to eat regularly with anyone who was available, agreeing to sit in the smoking section because everyone else was a smoker. The hours I spent taking notes on audiobooks in braille meant that I couldn't be picky about my friends. It was nice to just be accepted.

In time I contacted a Christian student group and asked for a ride to one of their meetings. This contact took all my courage. I wasn't just meeting new people. I was starting the first contact with the dreaded disclosure that I was blind, giving them the option to reject me.

The day came, and I dressed nicely. I waited. And waited. And waited.

An hour passed, and I gave up and changed out of my nice clothes. An hour and a half later, the contact person called. "I'm so sorry! I forgot! But we're still having fellowship. I can come pick you up. There's lots of food."

I agreed to go reluctantly. I was fairly sure that she had actually not forgotten but had instead decided not to come because I was blind. Memories of the girl at AU saying, "I can't escort you," ran through my head relentlessly.

Eventually I learned where the meetings were held, and I walked my own self if I wanted to. There would be no forgetting or rejecting.

STILL SEEKING SIGNS

I still had a lot of questions about healing. Why had I experienced improvement in my sight in 1992? Was it a partial healing? Or was it an accident of nature?

I decided during my first semester at SFA to ask the pastor of the small church I attended to anoint me and have the elders of the church pray for me. I still wanted complete healing, and I believed that I should follow the Biblical instructions in James 5:14-16 and profess my faith before the church.

The pastor refused to anoint me. I did not understand her reasoning, particularly when she began preaching sermons about faith in the spring of 1993. No one prayed for the sick people in the church. I began to feel very unsettled. How could I continue to grow in faith when I was attending a church where people did not exercise faith and the pastor clearly discouraged me from exercising mine?

WHO HAS THE TRUTH?

I decided that I needed to move to a new church where I could explore the topics of faith and healing freely. I began going to the local Assembly of God with a group of students from the Chi Alpha student group.

I wasn't sure what to expect. My memories of visiting Pentecostal churches as a teenager were not pleasant. I remembered a lot of babbling, and I remember feeling intense fear. To my surprise, I was very comfortable in this church. I liked the pastor's down-to-earth preaching style, and I loved the fact that the music was contemporary, and I could learn most of the songs easily. I could sing whether or not I had a hymnal! As much as I loved the robust hymn-singing in the Church of God where I grew up, I had never learned many of the hymns because the hymnal was not in braille. Most of the time, I stood quietly while everyone else did the thing I loved most: sing with all their being. I found the experience of singing music that had frequent repetition liberating.

After I left the Church of God, I received a call one day from an elderly lady. I thought that perhaps she might confront me about the fact that I had left some relationships unresolved when I stopped attending.

Instead, she asked, "Are you attending that Pentecostal church?"

I indicated that I was. This was perhaps a worse sin for some people than unresolved relationships. The Church of God (Anderson, IN) was decidedly not Pentecostal. Worshiping with the Pentecostals was about the worst thing one could do next to becoming a Baptist.

"Now," she said, "you know they sing that contemporary music, and we sing the old hymns. Now, I believe the old hymns have the truth."

I kept my mouth closed and listened; but I really wanted to ask if it wasn't the Bible and not the hymns that had the truth.

I don't remember how the conversation ended. I probably promised to think about what she said. But I probably thought about it differently from how she would have liked me to.

THE END OF PERSEVERANCE

I began to participate more fully in church activities. I joined the student worship team. Eventually, I gave my testimony, and the pastor anointed me and had the elders of the church lay hands on me. He explained that sometimes healing takes time, and I committed myself to wait patiently.

It did not come. I thought that perhaps I needed to persevere in asking; so, I allowed myself to be prayed over by various groups of people. Still, it did not come.

I disagreed strongly with the Assembly of God's position concerning speaking in tongues. Numerous times, I was told that the church believed that speaking in tongues was "the initial physical manifestation of the baptism of the Spirit." I wondered why it was necessary to look for physical manifestations at all. It seemed to me that this only led to boasting about one's ability to speak in tongues.

Eventually, I stopped discussing my theological differences. I wasn't going to change anyone's mind; and no one was going to change mine. I attended the church for several years but never joined.

My break with the Pentecostal church began to occur when I was invited to a prayer meeting held in someone's home.

The event was unlike any prayer meeting I had ever attended. It began with "spiritual warfare." Instead of praying, people shouted at "demons," telling them to "get out in the name of Jesus," and occasionally sang or shouted "Hallelujah." At one point, I found myself in the midst of the prayer circle, being prayed over. I have little memory of the event but suspect they probably were praying for my healing since they knew that I was open to such a thing. The prayer lasted a long time, and the people urged me repeatedly to shout, "Jesus!" I was crying violently and could not shout well—and really did not want to. I wanted to be left alone. I was overwhelmed and afraid; but I had no way of leaving. We were outside of town, and I did not know the address. I doubted anyone would have been able to hear me even if I could call someone to come and retrieve me.

I attended the meeting for a few days and then met with the pastor to ask his opinion of it. He strongly encouraged me not to attend any more meetings, saying that he did not condone these meetings and was very concerned about them. "I think those meetings are dangerous," he said. "I would advise you not attend any more!"

I did not return, explaining to the person who had invited me that I had homework to do. I appreciated the pastor's concern and recognized his maturity; but he was one person. I had been changed by these meetings; and my relationships with the members of the congregation suffered as a result.

I wondered what the person who prophesied that I would see by April thought when my birthday passed in May and I was still blind. Whose fault was it?

In spite of the trauma that I experienced, I continued attending the church for another year. When one has invested in relationships, it is difficult to leave a group, even when trauma is occurring. Leaving one group means starting over with a new group where there are no relationships.

PURITY

In the 1990s purity culture was probably a more important message for the Church to preach to young girls than the Gospel itself. Lest it seem heretical for me to say that, it is important for me to communicate the impact that it had on me as a female with a disability that impacted my ability to navigate independently.

The message to females, as I heard it, was that we must:

1. never tempt a man to sin;

2. never be alone with a man, because it creates the appearance of sin;

3. never tempt a man toward unfaithfulness from his spouse or girlfriend;

4. never be found in a situation which creates the appearance of unfaithfulness with a man

5. never ask anything of a man which creates the suggestion that you are proposing that he engage in a sinful act.

This meant that I could not accept a ride from a man, be guided by a man because I had accepted his arm; allow a man to meet with me at home for an appointment as an accommodation; or even meet with a male pastor at a public place that was familiar to me because it created the impression of accepting favors.

I struggled under the weight of purity culture for many years, first confronting it in the Pentecostal church when I realized that it was causing me to reject offers of transportation. I did not throw it off completely until many years later, when I was receiving pastoral counseling and I asked the pastor whether it wasn't wrong for him to meet me at my home. He explained that his staff knew where he was and expected him back in time for his next appointment. The staff circle of trust around us helped me to feel safe and honored. The weight of purity culture fell away from me as I realized that he had created a situation in which he could accommodate me safely.

In the meantime, I struggled to form healthy dating relationships. I never told anyone about my struggles, including the people I dated. I felt that the problem was me. When Kyle and I began dating in the mid-1990s, we did not have the resources or knowledge to confront this culture.

MY FINAL BREAK WITH PENTECOSTALISM

Several things led me to a final break with Pentecostalism. One probably had nothing to do with Pentecostalism itself, but because I was dependent on a limited number of people for transportation to church it was a powerful message to me whether it was intended to be or not.

At some point during my time at SFA, I moved into public housing for people with disabilities due to financial constraints. I did not communicate about my financial situation to anyone, thinking that it was my private business. My financial situation affected far more than my housing. I received food stamps and rationed my food.

I also could not afford to dry-clean my nice dresses. Doing so required a taxi trip to the dry-cleaner costing $5 each way, which was more than the cost of cleaning my dresses. So, my dresses lay on the floor in a bag, waiting for a chance to be cleaned, and I wore jeans to church.

One day when people picked me up for church, they asked rather irritably, "Why did you move all the way up here?"

I tried to explain without revealing my impoverished status that the complex had some services available for people with disabilities that I was able to use.

Then the woman said, "You do understand that people dress up for church on Sunday, don't you?" Shame filled my heart at the thought that she assumed that I had no respect for God! Throughout my life, my mom had explained to me that I didn't need to wear a dress every time the church was opened. I had said to her that I understood but I enjoyed being dressed up. We had had countless discussions about the fact that being overdressed could cause social difficulties for me. Now I was underdressed, and I could not talk about the reason why or do anything about it!

The most shameful part was yet to come.

Months later, I moved again due to some interpersonal difficulties within the disability complex. I found a roommate and moved to an apartment near campus. As it happened, I had a series of roommates before the end of my time in that apartment.

My last roommate in Texas was a person who had violent seizures. We learned much later that they were linked to severe panic attacks and social phobia, and with good mental health treatment she was able to learn to cope with her anxiety and participate in some social activities. When she lived with me, we knew only a few words that ended up causing a lot of pain because of the stigma that was associated with them.

We learned as we lived together that most people know how to beg God for healing. People know how to yell at demons and command them to get out of a person's life. Many people don't know how to be present with a person who has an illness that will not go away.

My friend wanted badly to go to church. She wanted the comfort of hearing that God was her help in the time of trouble. She wanted people to cry out for God's help with her, to call on God to be near to her.

She got something different.

We went down to the front so that she could kneel easily at the altar. But when she had a seizure, men carried her past everyone, out the back doors, and into a quiet room.

They didn't leave me with her and trust me to know what to do for her. They didn't even leave one man or one woman with me. They left three men with me: two elders and one medical professional.

The first time this happened, everyone prayed quietly. I appreciated the presence.

The second time it happened, the urgency of the prayers increased, as if the seizures were a problem that really must be fixed.

I began to sense the triggers for her seizures: mentions of hell, yelling, and too much loud music. We began sitting in the back, and I did my best to provide care quietly when I knew the seizures were coming. Sometimes all that happened was a shaking of the hand, and it stopped after I provided a few moments of gentle pressure. But other times, the handshaking escalated to a full-blown seizure. At those times, I tried to hold her in order to prevent her from throwing herself or hitting her head. The back row was truly a dangerous place for her to be.

Worst of all, when the men removed her again, more people began gathering, and they began to command demons to come out of her. Some of the people who began to gather in that quiet room were the people from the dangerous prayer meetings that I had stopped attending. I was powerless to make them stop their incantations. I couldn't ask the pastor for help—he was preaching. I begged God to make it stop, but all I could really do was wait it out and promise not to bring her back, not to do any more of what had been done to me.

In time we found another church. It didn't make the seizures stop, but it was a place where we were able to come to an understanding that no one would call for demons to come out and she could participate as she was able.

It would have helped if the Church had a healthy understanding of mental illness and had been an ally as we tried to advocate for effective treatment for her. The Pentecostal church was busy advocating for her to be off her meds or to be locked in the state hospital so that she would not be a negative influence on my life. The more of this I heard, the more distance I put between myself and Pentecostalism, and the more sternly I determined to be an advocate for people who could not advocate for themselves. My friend would not always live with me, but she would always be my friend, and I was not afraid of her illness.

DISAPPOINTMENTS AT SFA

Since I could not study music ministry at a state university, I tried my other love: teaching. I thought I had things well planned out. I would get a general teaching license with additional endorsements in visual impairment, special education, and ESL.

I took heavy courseloads. I deeply enjoyed my classes, including my internships in an ESL classroom and a class for children with learning disabilities. But one thing stood in my way.

When I went to my advisor's office to discuss plans for student teaching, she had strong words for me. "You will fail," she said.

"Why?" I asked. I'm doing fine in class, including yours."

"All blind people fail student teaching."

I listened to her defend her position for the next hour. Finally, I excused myself, saying I had another appointment. I wept openly as I made the 1.5-mile walk to another professor's office.

There was no evidence that any other blind person had failed student teaching, but my heart was already broken. I changed my major to psychology, supposing that if I had a four-year degree, I would be able to find a job of some kind. I was only one semester away from finishing my teaching degree, but what did it matter? I needed something I could succeed at.

TRYING TO BREATHE

During 1994 and 1995, I suffered several violent respiratory illnesses that doctors could not find an antidote for. In the fall of 1995, Kyle signed me into the hospital with fever, convulsions, and severe asthmatic bronchitis. I lashed out at him badly.

While shaking and trying to breathe under my covers, I hissed, "Why are you doing this!"

He calmly said, "The doctor will help you, and I'll be right here. You'll be better in a few days" He also called my parents, who came to visit me.

Blood tests showed that I had a bacterial pneumonia called mycoplasma. I was treated with IV antibiotics, steroids, and nebulized medication for asthma.

After leaving the hospital, I saw a doctor for allergy testing. On the day of testing, I lay on a table and had my back pricked with test needles. Then I waited for 30 minutes to see which of the test spots developed a reaction.

After 30 minutes, the doctor and nurse came back in. "Oh, goodness! I should've brought my camera!" the doctor exclaimed. "That's the biggest corn reaction I've ever seen in my life!"

For several months, I went to the doctor each week for allergy shots. They must have helped to some degree. I was not sick for three years. However, eventually the chronic infections returned with a vengeance. They have been with me for most of my adult life; and I have used inhalers and nebulized medications at home since 2001.

LIFE CHANGES

Prior to changing my major, I worked up to 20 hours a week taking notes for students with learning disabilities. In 1996, I added another thing to my plate. Kyle and I got married. We had met through the Christian student group. We were both very young; and the marriage was very poorly planned. We did not attend extensive marriage counseling. Later we learned that we had completely conflicting priorities in life.

Our failure to attend marriage counseling was rooted in difficulties we had with the Pentecostal church. When we revealed our intent to be married, the campus pastor told us that we were being rebellious toward God and tried to find someone to counsel us who knew something about blindness. Neither of us could figure out what blindness had to do with getting marriage counseling from a pastor. So, we asked a family member to perform the wedding.

Counseling that provided solid guidance about the impact of marrying without having chosen stable life plans might have helped us. A safe place to talk about our anxieties, hopes, and dreams and places where they might have conflicted certainly would have helped. These things didn't have to do with blindness. They had to do with being young people in college.

We separated after 13 months and divorced after an additional year. In time, we spoke honestly about the problems in our marriage. We are both healthier today because of those conversations.

PART-TIME WORK, OR NOT

During the mid-1990s, I decided that I wanted to work off-campus. I put in several job applications and finally landed an interview with a medical answering service. I thought that surely this job would not be difficult. It should be like other phone work I had done, and by this time the Americans with

Disabilities Act should hold some power for people with disabilities. I learned differently when a person from church took me to apply for the job.

We arrived, and I began to get myself and my dog out of his car. Suddenly I heard angry shouting and realized that a lady was at the door, yelling at us to leave.

"I'm here to apply for the answering service job," I said nicely.

"You have to be able to READ to do this job!" the lady shouted.

"I can read," I said. "I have a laptop that talks. The ADA…"

"I know all about the ADA. We have employees in wheelchairs! But you have to be able to READ!"

Having gotten the point that one needed to be able to read with actual eyes, I shoved my dog back into the car, made sure her tail was in, and slammed the door.

"Would you like me to take you somewhere? Would you like a burger or something?" asked the person from church. I barely knew his name. He had heard me ask for prayer about the interview and offered to drive so that I wouldn't need to spend the money on a taxi. I was so grateful that I hadn't taken a taxi! But at the moment, the last thing I wanted was to be in a car with any other person. What I would not give to be able to drive, alone, and let my makeup run, all by myself.

"No, thank you. Please just take me home," I said, turning to the window as the sobbing began in earnest.

After changing my major to psychology, I withdrew from work and extracurricular activities. My withdrawal reflected my belief that there was no hope for me to participate successfully in society. I wish now that I had confided in someone.

I went to SFA with hopes of transitioning to adulthood successfully. At the end of my time there, I felt that I had failed in every attempt I had made. There was one bright spot in my life.

Not long after Kyle and I were married, he went home to spend Easter with his mom. While he was there, he called to talk to me. "Guess what I'm holding," he said.

I heard a tiny mewing.

"My sister's cat had kittens," he said. "Aren't they cute?"

I thought, on one hand, how cute! On the other, how cruel for him to let me hear a kitten, knowing that I couldn't have one in our apartment. I kept my thoughts of irritation to myself.

Several months later, his mother and sister visited during the weekend that we were getting ready to move to a new apartment. They brought two kittens: a black one for me and a gray tabby for my friend who was moving out of my apartment. My black kitten, Inca, was my companion for the next seventeen years.

21

THE GRAY CURTAIN RETURNS

In the spring of 1998, I moved back in with my parents after separating from Kyle. When I arrived home, I realized that I could no longer see the lights in my childhood house. How long had this been going on? When had I stopped seeing anything but the brightest sunlight?

I tried at first to blame circumstances at my parents' home. They were planning to move from Texas to Indiana, and when I arrived home there were numerous boxes stacked throughout the house. But the truth was that I should have been able to see brown cardboard boxes.

"Put your hand in front of you," my dad suggested.

In my mind, I heard a great terrorized scream. "NOOOOO!!!!!" I envisioned the little child self dragging her leg along the grass at the Texas School for the Blind, no longer free to run and tumble. I couldn't even walk through a house by myself!

I made an appointment with my childhood ophthalmologist. I had not seen him since 1992, and I was a bit nervous.

When he came into the office, he greeted me warmly and tried looking into my eye with his trusty ophthalmoscope. As hard as I tried to keep the eye open, great tears rained down my face, and the eye reflexively closed. On one hand this was promising. It showed that I was reacting to light. On the other hand, it prevented him from seeing inside my eye.

He tipped the chair back and left the room briefly to retrieve another piece of equipment. When he returned, he said, "I've got my wrestling shoes."

My pressure had crept up to a dangerous level again, and my cornea was scarred. He left me with a new set of drops and encouraged me to find another ophthalmologist after the move who could perform a cornea transplant. "It's possible that something could be done for your retina," he said.

The new combination of drops was successful at lowering the pressure, and my vision improved slightly. But on most days things continued to appear through that gray curtain which only glaring sunlight could easily penetrate.

THE LONG WAIT FOR TREATMENT

Many things needed to be arranged in Indiana before I could begin the process of finding a doctor. I needed to transfer my Social Security checks there and apply for Medicaid. While all that was happening, I needed somehow to stay on my glaucoma medication—without a doctor to prescribe it. Once I had Medicaid, I could begin the process of finding a doctor who was willing to provide treatment for an adult with such little sight. While I waited, I would have to live with the gray curtain.

I became curious about what was happening to my eyes. My dad and I packed up my big, bulky scanner and spent the day at the medical library, scanning articles and book chapters into a portable disk drive.

I found and joined an email support group for people with ROP and their families. For the first time in my life, I talked freely about my vision loss and the feelings I was experiencing.

The process of transferring my Social Security payments did not go well. I called to provide my change of address by the required due date; but it was not entered on time. This resulted in a delay in my check being sent to Indiana. A representative suggested that I go to the post office in Texas to pick it up.

After we moved, I went to the family services office and applied for Medicaid. After I had settled my dog guide in front of my chair, the caseworker asked why I needed Medicaid. "Are you blind or something?" she asked in a syrupy tone.

I was stunned. Did she not understand why I had a dog guide or why I was wearing glasses bigger than anyone's best magnifier? I simply answered, "Yes."

The caseworker's tone devolved to a level generally reserved for preschoolers. "We'll need some information from your doctor," she said. "If you're blind enough, you'll be able to have Medicaid." She stressed the words "blind enough" as if they were a special status and surely, I was too stupid to know what "bliiiiind enough" meant. She had no idea how long the application would take or how I should get my medications in the meantime.

Two months later, I finally received my Medicaid card. By this time, a friend who was part of the email ROP group had told me about a doctor, Michael Trese, in Michigan, who was an expert on ROP. I decided that if he could take Indiana Medicaid, I would like to see him. My decision was confirmed after a local doctor said that he would only recommend two doctors in the state of Indiana to perform a cornea transplant for me. The cornea transplant was the easy part. He had no recommendations for retina specialists with appropriate expertise to work on my very damaged retina.

Dr. Trese agreed with the recommendation for a cornea transplant and possible retina surgery. He referred me to a cornea specialist in a nearby office, who agreed to do the transplant. I would need to travel to Detroit for each follow-up appointment.

While waiting for my eye surgery, I was also coping with changes in my relationship with my dog. Elli had begun to be less tolerant of long working days. In fact, I could walk faster than she could most of the time. I retired her officially when I realized that she would not enjoy the active lifestyle I wanted to lead once my healing was complete. I also decided that I would not put in an application for a new dog right away.

22

STOLEN GIFTS

In late 1998, I began to look for a new church to attend. One day in December, I returned to my parents' large church for a repeat visit. I felt that it was important to visit a church several times before making a commitment. This particular visit made a profound impression on me.

On this particular morning, I was with a university student who was also new to the church. My dad had dropped the two of us off and gone to park the car.

An older lady greeted me, handed me a bulletin, and made a rather loud comment about me having someone read it to me later. I felt irritated and wondered why she couldn't just say welcome.

We stepped inside and found a place to wait for my dad. I felt very uncomfortable after having been greeted in such a manner. I would have appreciated some words of welcome, an introduction, something to make me feel at home. Instead, I had been instructed on how to handle my difference as if I didn't know what to do. I felt more shut out than ever.

After my friend and I stood waiting for a few moments, The greeter came up again. "Where do you get talking books for the blind?" she asked, drawing her words out slowly.

Where was my welcome? What was her name? I was still cold from being outside! I had only lived here for four months! I didn't know the answer to what she was asking. But to admit that I didn't know would make me appear more helpless than I already seemed! This was awful! Where was my dad?

A little child suddenly broke into my panicked thoughts, saying loudly, "Oh, she's BLIND!" His mom said, equally loudly "I guess not."

My dad finally arrived and saved the day by guiding me into the auditorium. Still, I could not quiet my heart and mind. All I could think about was the sound of the child shouting, "She's BLIND!!!" as if he had discovered a dinosaur.

Then someone began to read:

"Jesus. Tiny Jesus…"

She spoke softly and tenderly, pronouncing the words with great clarity and awe, as if calling upon my very soul to listen.

I recognized her voice. Her name was Jennifer Jones, and she was commonly known as J.J. She was an old friend from my undergraduate years at AU.

She was a conversation partner for me when I studied French. She came into my dorm room one day, saw me writing a letter in print to a friend and commented on its legibility. "Hey, I can read that!" She loved my dog at a time when some students couldn't stand being around dogs. She had a distinct style of speaking that always made me feel calm, even when my world was falling apart.

As she finished the reading, she invited the children to go out of the sanctuary for their worship time. I whispered to my dad urgently, "I need to see her!" He agreed to go with me to look for her but said that he doubted we could find her.

After church, an older lady came and spoke to me. "It's Jeanne Blocker."

I remembered her with great happiness. She and her husband transported me to church when I was an undergraduate student at AU. Her soft speech comforted me.

My dad and I were successful in locating J.J. She and I exchanged phone numbers, and I felt that the church trip was not quite as awful as it first seemed.

STEALING GIFTS

People often suggest that I think of questions like those the greeter asked as opportunities to minister. Ministry is an act of giving, of intentional empowerment to others. Even Jesus did not permit people to take from him when he had the power to heal. When the woman with the flow of blood touched the hem of his garment and intended to go unnoticed, he reordered the situation so that she identified herself and he was in a position to give to her by his initiative. He also needed times of aloneness and personal support. When he prayed in the garden of Gethsemane, three of his disciples kept watch (albeit falling asleep). No one approached him to ask for healing favors or miracles.

On that morning, I wanted simply to be a person. I wanted to be welcome in the church. I was not in a good space for questions at the time. I was afraid and lonely. I badly needed some ministry. But I did not feel like a person. I felt like an information bank. I felt that I had no right to say, "I don't know, and I don't want to talk about this." I wrote in my journal:

> *I must have compassion, and my compassion must be perfect and ever ready. It doesn't matter if I'm hurting or whether I feel like talking about it or not.*

> *...I feel like every aspect of who I am which makes me different—less able—than others can be examined as if it is fascinating. I am a symbol of the blind, pitied or condescendingly admired, never related to on a personal level. I have no being other than my blindness. If I had it, wouldn't it be seen?*

I did not tell anyone at the church about the experience. I wanted to. But if they addressed the issue with the greeters, the lady's feelings would have been hurt.

In my journal, I lamented the fact that people often question me about blindness when it might otherwise be considered rude to engage a person: while I'm having other conversations, while I'm eating dinner with a friend, while I'm reading, sometimes even while I am crying...Sometimes people become offended when I refuse to answer a very personal question. For me to insist on being treated with common courtesy, even in the most polite way, is often seen as unacceptable.

The only thing about me which seems to be treated as private is often the thing which I want most to share: my real self.

Is it any wonder that people with disabilities have difficulty in discerning what is appropriate to share and not to share!

There are many ways in which we steal things from others instead of allowing them to give willingly to us from the stores of their joy and resources. I am not immune from this behavior just because I know how it feels when people do it to me. Instead of identifying our need openly and allowing the other person to respond as they are able, we hoard what we want from them. As I lament my own experience, I work to be more compassionate in my interactions with others. Is it really the best time to ask that person my question about what they have spent all day doing as a job? Sometimes just the question, "Is this a good time to talk about something?" feels good.

FINDING A BALANCE IN CHURCH

It is true that I will never find the perfect church experience. Church is a place where all kinds of people come seeking to encounter Jesus. I will encounter them on the way, and I will experience their reactions to me. I am also flawed, and people will encounter me along their way.

Painful experiences can activate the traumatic response that results in a person pulling away from church. On the other hand, acts that engage people emotionally and call them deeply to listen and continue to seek an authentic experience with Christ and with the community are extremely powerful. Every person doesn't go into a new church with a previous history of relationships with the community, so it may be hard to make those initial connections. It is not the seeker's responsibility to do this but the community's responsibility to engage and call the seeker toward relationship. I thank God for Jeanne and J.J., who did this for me at that difficult time in my life.

23

THE EXPERIENCE
OF BLINDNESS

As I prepared for surgery in 1998, I expected to put up with several months without any sight at all. Instead, my sight came and went without any predictability. I might see nothing but painful glare from the sun. I might see pinpoints of light from behind a gray haze. Occasionally I might see an object! I was surprised one day when I pointed to a small dark object on the ground while I was out with my sister. She said casually, "Oh, it's a squirrel."

I had difficulty sleeping because so many thoughts raced through my head. What would happen when I woke up from surgery? Would light pour in as it had when I was a child and overwhelm me? Would I be able to see and recognize things I had seen during my childhood? Would I be able to see my own face in a mirror? I hadn't seen that since I was around ten years old.

I always had a very small amount of sight in comparison to people with normal sight. I could not read print or drive during my teens or young adulthood. I could not see faces. These are things I did not miss since they aren't part of my general life experience. The idea of seeing a face was a curiosity and not a need.

I did miss the things that were part of my life experience: recognizing familiar places and objects, being able to trust my eyes to give me reliable information about my environment, etc. These things changed the way that I lived and interacted with the world.

On some days my memories of seeing were very clear. On other days I was afraid that I would forget what seeing was like....I also had emotional appreciation for colors and memories associated with environmental settings.

Some of my visual memories are just plain entertaining. There are no words to describe my thoughts as I went out into the back yard one day and counted seventeen huge mushrooms with my very own eyes. I could not see the stems. I could only see the huge round white tops. I wanted to touch one. I wanted to know if they were fuzzy....In a moment of excitement, I pointed to a pink rubber ball and said, "There's another one!"

LIVING WITH THE GRAY CURTAIN

I didn't have any idea in 1998 that I would experience the loss of sight again and again and again. I thought that I would have surgery, and it would make things all better. I thought that, having learned my lesson about the glaucoma drops, I would simply be a good girl this time and things would be fine from now on.

The experience of sight loss was not always the same. I could not always describe it clearly. But I always knew when it was happening because the gray curtain always returned. I wished every time that I could just tell the doctor, "The gray curtain is back."

In time I learned how to tell the doctor things that indicated that surgery had been useful: "I'm not running into walls anymore." "I can locate objects on the floor." "I can see the differences in the color of objects even though I can't match the name of colors." "I can pick out clothing in the store that has color patterns that are pleasing to me." "I picked out the color of paint for the walls in our new house."

These might seem like small, everyday things, but for me they were monumental things that I had not done even as a child. I had never tried to pick out clothing by color. I assumed I couldn't do it because I "just had light perception". Having surgery on my eyes as an adult forced me to explore the limits of what "light perception" actually meant in terms of my personal life. It often meant more than what could be documented in a medical chart.

24

AFTER SURGERY

I was not alert enough to feel the pain. I could only hear a woman yelling, "Give me a phone! I've gotta get out of here!" Her voice came from across the room and to my right. I supposed there must be several beds in the recovery room. I remembered nothing of this part of previous hospital stays. Already I did not want to remember this one.

A nurse tried to explain to the woman that she could not leave. "You've been in a car accident, ma'am," she said. "You have a broken leg."

"I've gotta get out of here," the woman insisted.

I drifted off to sleep again, thinking how horrible it was that a person could not suffer her physical traumas alone in peace and quiet, unsure whether I wished the quiet for myself or the lady with the broken leg, and hoping that the poor woman with the broken leg was not my roommate.

When I woke up again a couple of hours later, I was in my own room. My mother was sitting beside me, and she was talking with an elderly lady in the next bed. I needed to go to the bathroom. I made several unsuccessful attempts to communicate with Mom. My voice was gone, probably from being intubated during the surgery— and I was still very weak. I had not eaten in over twenty-four hours.

Finally, I succeeded in getting Mom's attention. "Bathroom," I whispered, expecting her to call the nurse to bring a bed pan.

Instead, she got up, helped me get out of bed, and walked with me to the bathroom, pulling my IV pole along behind me.

By this time, I had begun to be aware of the patch over my right eye and the annoying, indescribable itching behind it. I climbed back into my bed. I wanted to read my Braille magazine, but I was too weak and restless to concentrate. I wiggled around into a more comfortable position on my left side. As I was falling asleep, a nurse came in.

"Are you having any pain?" she asked. "Do you need more Morphine?"

Morphine? I thought other medications were used after eye surgery—things like Vicodin. Two scenes flashed quickly through my mind. I remembered watching an episode of "Little House on the Prairie" in which Albert was addicted to Morphine. His addiction was discovered after he had begun to be hostile and fell asleep in school. I remembered the scenes depicting his violent illness during withdrawal.

Then I remembered my grandmother's last few weeks of life. She had been given Morphine to ease the pain from the cancer which had invaded her body. I remembered standing at her bedside as her breathing slowed until it was no more. I wasn't sure what morphine would do to me, and I wasn't sure I wanted to find out. I wasn't even sure whether to call the annoying scratchy sensation pain.

"I'll just give you a little bit," the nurse said kindly. "It's about time for another dose."

Oh, what was this? Was there some schedule for doling out Morphine? I opened my braille watch and checked the time. It was 11:00 PM, two hours after I had supposedly come into my room. What would Morphine do to me, anyway?

Mom sat beside my bed, reading a magazine. My roommate asked for some Vicodin, and the nurse left. I rolled over onto my left side, too tired to read my braille magazine but too anxious to rest. Did I have this surgery in vain? If my small amount of vision was restored, what would things look like?

Suddenly, the scratchy feeling behind the patch was gone. Before I had much time to marvel over this, I fell into a blissful sleep....Morphine must be a good drug after all!

I woke up again about two hours later. The annoying sensation was back, but I was too groggy to tell anyone. It was tolerable, so I just turned over and tried to sleep on my back. I was restless. I pushed the button at the side of the bed to raise my head slightly.

I assumed the nurse would come in soon to see if I needed more Morphine. It was probably about time for another dose, if my calculation was right. I supposed I was being given Morphine every two hours as needed.

I was right. I nodded when she asked if I wanted the Morphine. Soon I felt the sleepiness coming and the scratchy feeling subsiding. As I drifted off, I thought of the coming morning when the patch would be removed, and my eye would be examined. Mom had said the surgery went well. But what did that mean? Fleeting thoughts of articles describing surgeries resulting in retinal reattachment but no return of vision passed through my mind. What if I became the subject of one of those articles? What if my vision didn't return? Had I done the right thing? Was I feeling this strange sensation for no good reason?

I was glad to have the surgery over after so many months of waiting and planning. A doctor had recommended it eight months earlier, but I had put it off because my family was in the midst of a cross-country move. After the move, I waited several months before seeing Dr. Trese, who agreed to evaluate my retina during surgery and perform a vitrectomy, if possible, to reattach any detached portions. At the least, I would have a cornea transplant.

The doctors could not estimate the potential benefits of the surgery. In fact, the cornea specialist was not at all positive and stressed the fact that I would need to follow his instructions during the recovery period, even if the surgery failed.

The decision was a difficult one to make. Did I really want to go through this kind of pain and discomfort if I wouldn't get any benefit from it? I finally decided that I would rather have the surgery and know for sure that there was no chance of regaining the vision I had lost than to always wonder if anything could have been done. Now, eight long months of searching and waiting had come to an end. The surgery would fail or succeed, and no one could control it. Either way, it would soon be time to move on to a new phase of my life.

Early in the morning, another nurse came to give me eye drops. I had never liked eye drops, and this time was no exception. My eye would not open on its own. Most of the medicine ran down my cheek instead of into my eye, And the scratchy feeling was actually painful now.

I ate a big breakfast of eggs, biscuits, and bacon; and the nurse removed my IV. Then I dressed and walked with Mom to the examining room where the ophthalmologist was waiting. The gauze had been removed from my patch, and through the holes in the shield I could see blurry shapes in the hallway.

The doctor examined me briefly. I tried hard not to squint against the tiny, piercing light which told me that perhaps the surgery had been successful. He explained that things would look very blurry for a while during the recovery process and that I would experience changes in my vision for several months.

Mom took me back to my room, and I prepared to leave. A nurse gave me a plastic box with gauze pads, several rolls of tape, and several bottles of eye drops to take home. I would be using drops several times a day for over a year. The nurse also told me that I must wear a shield while I slept, and during the day I must wear the shield or my glasses to prevent anything from bumping or getting into my eye.

Soon we were on our way home. I slept soundly during the five- hour drive. I needed that sleep; for a fascinating and emotional journey lay ahead. Oh yes, and the itching was going to continue for a while—without Morphine.

RECOVERY AT HOME

I held the tissue in my hand and stared. Its color had caught my attention as I was pulling it away after blotting a drop of excess medication from my eye. White was one of the few colors I had learned to recognize as a child. How long had it been since I had known anything was white?

I laid the eye shield aside and reached for my glasses. With my glasses on, I stared at the top of the dresser. I saw objects of different shapes and sizes. I began to touch them, trying to make sense out of what I was seeing. I tried to conjure up the memories of similar objects from my childhood.

Sitting in the chair near my lamp, I took off my white tennis shoe and tossed it, watching it sail across the room. I repeated the process with my other shoe and then peeled off my socks, shut my eyes, and tossed them. As I scanned the floor to see where they had landed, I felt like a little child.

I had a recording of myself playing with light-colored plastic eggs that could be taken apart and put back together. I took the eggs apart, threw the halves on the floor, and laughed with glee. I imagine myself watching them fall to the floor just as I was watching my shoes and socks at this moment.

On the tape, my mother came into the room, saw what I had done, and said, "Sarah Jane, you pick up all these eggs right now!" And I picked up all the eggs, singing with joy as I went along.

No one comes in to tell me to pick up my socks and shoes. But I feel a bit like singing as I retrieve them.

"Things will look much different in a few months," the doctor had told me before he released me from the hospital. "Your vision will be a bit cloudy because of the gas bubble, but your cornea is clear, and we expect you'll see some improvement over several months."

Several months! I couldn't imagine what things would be like several months down the road. Already I was seeing things I hadn't seen in many years.

I got up from my chair and went out into the living room. On the way, I passed the dining room table, and some papers lying on it caught my eye. Papers! When had I last seen papers?

In the living room, I stood near the television, mesmerized by the moving images. I tried in vain to identify something, even a color. I could not; and the images made me feel nauseated.

I headed back to my bedroom to put the patch on my eye. I wanted to be in the dark. My mind was overwhelmed by visual stimulation after living almost completely without it for the past eight months. Over time I would become accustomed to it and spend more time looking at things. For now, I needed rest. I discovered new things to see every day. I became almost addicted to looking at new things, and I had to remind myself when I became overwhelmed that everything would still be there for me to see after I had rested. I could identify with Sheila Hocken's feelings following the removal of congenital cataracts at age 30, as described in her book, *Emma and I.*

> I kept thinking, "If those colors were so beautiful, what about the rest, what about everything else?" The colors were still dancing and whirling about in my mind behind the bandages, changing pattern as in a child's kaleidoscope, and exploding like fireworks. What was it like outside? I wanted to tear the bandages off and rush to the window and see everything.

I wanted to share my discoveries, but I could find few words to describe the experience of seeing again. I looked at each new object or picture and thought, "It's really here, and it really has color!" Sharing the experience happened only through behaviors. One night as I was eating dinner, my mom noticed that I was looking at my plate and choosing where to pick up food with my fork. "Can you see that?" she exclaimed. I couldn't remember ever choosing food from my plate by looking at it.

WHAT NOT TO WATCH

My parents went back to work a day or two after my surgery, and I was home alone during the months that followed. One afternoon, I stood in front of the TV, staring at bright colors and flashes of light, thinking I was watching a replay of a fireworks display.

Suddenly, I tuned in to the dialogue and was shocked to discover that I was watching a documentary about Desert Storm! My stomach churned violently, and I turned the TV off. When my mother arrived home a few minutes later, I was still standing in front of a black screen, sobbing loudly.

"Is something wrong with your eye?" Mom asked.

I shook my head.

"What's wrong?"

I don't remember if I ever was able to tell her. I have never stood in front of a TV since then, though I am still curious about what I might be able to see on the screen.

"CAN YOU SEE ME?"

Perhaps the most fascinating thing for me was looking at people. I could recall seeing some facial features as a child; but after my surgery, I was fascinated anew by faces.

Because my vision was still so limited, my exposure to faces was limited to those people who stood within a foot or two of me while we talked—or children I held in my arms. My four-year-old niece took great delight in climbing up into my arms, pressing her face close to mine, and asking, "Can you see me?" Although Harmony did not yet understand what blindness really meant, I think the fact that I could now see her face fascinated her as much as it did me. She had beautiful dark skin, and I would have looked at her all day if I could have held her so long.

Some people expressed uncertainty upon hearing of my interest in faces. "What if I look like Frankenstein?" asked one friend who was blind.

I realized then that I had entered the world of people who can judge based on appearance. Not only that, but because I could see, my friend who feared looking like Frankenstein was more vulnerable before me than I was before him. This revelation humbled me, and I wanted him to understand that seeing his face was for me a new way to affirm something I already believed. He was my dear friend, perfectly unique and wonderful just the way he was.

PERCEPTION AND REALITY

During the first weeks after the surgery in 1998, my eyes were dilated with Atropine so that the movement of the iris would not cause pain during the time when my eye was sensitive. I experienced a pattern of light sensitivity followed by adjustment and visual improvement similar to the pattern I had experienced in 1992.

I had forgotten about this pattern, and when the brightness began to fade after the first week, I became afraid that I was experiencing visual loss and should report it. I also began to experience urges to harm myself. These urges were frightening to me. I had no rational desire to harm myself. After I realized that I was following my normal pattern of recovery, I expected the urges to subside, assuming that they had somehow been related to the fear of vision loss.

The urges did not subside. I began to look for information about my eye medications online. I also called the optometrist who had taught a course I took about eye anatomy and pathology. He was very alarmed to know that I was taking Atropine and told me that it could cause a number of neurological problems as well as severe depression.

I began to write down the times when I took my various medications and the times when the urges to harm myself were most intense. Finally, I was able to see that the urges were strongest about two hours after I had taken the Atropine. I obtained permission to stop the Atropine, and the urges vanished. I relaxed and began to enjoy the positive results of the surgery.

I continued to experience visual improvement for several months. I was amazed at some of the small objects I could see. My parents shared in my amazement as I discovered that I could locate individual bites of food on my plate and watch ground beef change from red to brown as it cooked. I kept family and friends informed via an online journal, exclaiming over small things like the food on my plate as well as big things like the first snow on New Year's Day, 1999.

Regaining vision is in some ways similar to losing it. It requires a person to adjust and cope with different kinds of input. I had no assistance with this adjustment process, and I found very little information in books or on the Internet about people whose sight had been restored or adjustment to sight restoration. Charlotte Sanford and Sheila Hocken's books were comforting to me, and I found a couple of old books and articles about "visual rehabilitation." However, none of these resources provided real guidance in just how to go about learning to use my vision for me.

I needed to learn all over again how to use my eyes and how to interpret what I was seeing. I learned most things through trial and error. Because I did not know how reliable my vision was, and because I had lived so much of my life with less vision, I relied heavily on my sense of touch to confirm anything I thought I saw. While browning meat, I relied on the texture and smell of the meat while watching the change in color. When I saw an object on a table, I touched it in order to identify it.

The most difficult aspect of adjusting to the restored vision was the difference between my perception and my memories. While preparing for surgery, I had basked in memories of colors and objects, noting every detail of the memory from the size of the object to the brightness of the color. However, what I saw after surgery often did not look like what I remembered seeing as a child. Since I lived with my parents, I was exposed to many of the same objects which I had seen during my childhood and adolescence. I relied on visual memory to help me make sense of what I was seeing now; and I was troubled by the inconsistency. Furthermore, I was troubled by my reaction to the concept of losing my vision. Struggling to make sense of my thoughts, I wrote them down in my journal.

> *I'm kind of disappointed. Things don't look like I thought they would look. They don't look like I remember them looking. This doesn't mean I am regretful, but it does mean that I'm having to somehow reconcile the differences between my memories and the present. Does the table look like it looks now, or does it look like it looked back then? And now that I am old enough to understand that there is a difference, is the table supposed to look like it looks to me, or is it supposed to look like what other people see?*

> *Questions like these really drive home the point that reality is not what we see. What we see is merely a certain perception of reality which can change. I've questioned my reasons for having the surgery and my reasons for having difficulty with vision loss. It wasn't so much that I could not live with the loss. I could. What was I trying to hold on to? My perception of reality? Something from my past in a time when I was leaving a lot of my past behind me? Something that would somehow help me to make sense of all these other changes? If I could see the table and realize that it looked the same as it did yesterday or last week, would it help me*

to make sense of the fact that it is still the same table even
though it is in a different house?

…I am and have always been a very visually oriented person
in spite of not having much to work with. When I organize
a mental map, I see the images in my mind and rearrange
them. Of course, I'm rearranging my own perceptions of
images, but it is still a visual process. I am not automati-
cally rerouted to using tactual or auditory processing meth-
ods, even though I do both of these quite well. Losing the
vision was more an issue of losing the input into my pre-
ferred channel of processing than an issue of losing the abil-
ity to function in the world. I held onto something—a set
of memories of what things "were supposed to look like"—
and put all my hope in this surgery. Things would return
to "normal" after the surgery. Everything would look right.
And it isn't that way. Some things do, and some things don't.
Why? I will never know. It's just the way it is.

Over time, I adjusted to the conflict between memory and
the present, and I built a new frame of reference based on the
present. I asked Dr. Trese whether he thought I might be able
to learn to read very large print and identify objects visually
again. He said that most people could not learn these things
with such a small amount of vision but that I might be able to
with self-discipline.

One thing hampered my progress in learning to use my vision.
I was prone to temporary vision loss which could indicate that
my body was rejecting the cornea. I was to report any vision

loss and see the doctors very soon. However, I was often uncertain whether I had lost vision or whether some aspect of the environment—lighting, weather, or even my own fatigue—had changed and was causing me to have difficulty seeing. I eventually learned to evaluate visual loss not only by assessing the contrast I could perceive but also by noting my ability to locate specific types of objects. This enabled me to know when I needed to report changes in my visual functioning. It also allowed me to set fear aside and enjoy some things I had never seen before.

STARS

"There's only one star in the sky," Judi told me as we drove along, the motion of the car lulling her 18-month-old grandson to sleep. "I wish you could see it!"

I shifted anxiously in the passenger seat. The baby was quiet in his car seat behind me. I felt that I should say something, but I did not know what to say. Judi and I had been corresponding via email for a year because of something she had seen on my Web site, but only recently had we discussed my blindness in detail. Now, on the first day I had spent with her in person, she was wishing I could see a star. I didn't know how to respond.

I had seen the moon a handful of times in my life, but never had I seen a star. Although I was curious about THEM, the fact that I could not see them did not upset me. The only thing that upset me was the feeling of inferiority I sometimes had when my inability to see meant that I could not share an experience with others. As I tried to think of something to say, I wondered if Judi would be disappointed or consider me inferior if I could not see the star.

"What if we drove out in the country where there were no streetlights?" Judi asked. "Do you think maybe you could see it then?"

I shifted again in my seat. She really wanted me to see this star! How could I tell her there was no way I could ever see it? Even after a surgery which had enabled me to see things I had never seen before, I still could see no more than ten feet in front of me. How could I see a star?

Reluctantly, I agreed that we could try it. It couldn't hurt anything. I just didn't want to imagine seeing something that I could not really see. Some of my friends with visual impairments had told me that they often found themselves pretending to see things they really could not see in order to please their family and friends. I couldn't do that to Judi. We would just drive into the country, and I would take a look and be honest with her about not seeing the star.

As we drove, memories flashed quickly through my mind. I remembered the first time I had seen the moon. I had been with my father, out in the driveway in front of our home. He stood behind me and put his hands on either side of my head, guiding my face in the right direction. I hadn't expected to see anything then. It was just an experiment. Instead of nothing, I had seen a pale, glowing ball. I wondered if a star would look at all like the moon.

Now, just three months after my surgery, I was riding out into the country to look for a star. Secretly, I hoped that perhaps her idea would prove fruitful, but I maintained a fairly high degree of skepticism.

Judi stopped the car and turned off the engine and the head-lights. We got out, and I was struck by the silence of the night. I grew up in Houston, and I could not remember a time when I had not heard the noise of passing cars, sirens, or airplanes.

We walked away from the car. Judi stood behind me, just as my father had done the first time we looked at the moon. She turned my face upwards, just as he had done, and I prepared to tell her that I saw nothing.

But what was that tiny pinpoint of light far away? I couldn't believe it! I must have been wrong. I closed my eyes and then looked again, trying to convince myself that it was not there. But there it was, shining steadily.

"Can you see it?" she asked, a bit of excitement in her voice.

I felt as if I could shout, if only my breath wasn't taken away by the inexplicable joy inside me. "I've never seen a star!" I exclaimed. "I wasn't going to let you stop the car. I didn't think I could have seen it." I embraced her, nearly bursting into tears.

Judi and I went star gazing one more night that week. I thought that I surely had imagined the star the first night. If it happened again, I would be amazed.

Again, we drove out into the country. This time I searched more independently, and again I expected nothing. I was amazed to discover two or three groups of pinpoints, more pale than the one I had seen the first night. I closed my eyes and turned them away. When I opened them again and turned back toward the place, the groups of pinpoints shone like little groups of candles hanging from the sky. In one group, a single pinpoint shone brighter than the others, catching my attention.

When Judi and I first discussed stars, I asked her if they really had five or six points. More than anything, I wanted to understand what a star was. It did not matter to me whether I understood it by seeing it or by receiving an explanation. She answered that they appeared that way if she squinted. Her matter-of-fact answer to my question and willingness to answer other questions flooded me with a feeling of fellowship and removed all feelings of inferiority that came from the knowledge of my physical difference. In that moment, I realized that whether or not I ever saw a star or even another object, I was a part of God's family and I could be amazed at His handiwork along with everyone else.

For many years I found it difficult to sing the lines of a certain hymn:

> *I see the stars, I hear the rolling thunder,*
> *Thy power throughout the universe displayed.*
> *Then sings my soul, my Savior God, to thee.*
> *How great thou art! How great thou art!*[5]

Judi's willingness to explain the appearance of the stars freed me to praise God for His works in the heavens. Whether or not I had seen the stars, I would have been at peace with my blindness at that time. But God knows the desires of my heart and blesses me every so often with a gift I never expected to receive. I have never seen stars again; but I treasure the memory of those two occasions.

---

5. Carl Boberg, "How Great Thou Art." 1886.

THE FOUR DREADED WORDS

The first indication that something was wrong came just a few weeks after surgery. I had an upper respiratory infection and lost some vision.

I traveled to Detroit, where I saw both doctors. Neither was very concerned, and Dr. Trese said that the vision would probably improve when I got well.

He was right, and a few weeks later I saw the stars at night for the first time in my life. Yet still my uneasiness grew.

I continued to have chronic upper respiratory infections, and I continued to experience vision loss. Usually it seemed temporary, but when the infections were gone and the vision returned, I always noticed that it was not quite as clear as it had been before the infection. By December 1999, I had lost all of my vision. I scheduled another trip to Detroit.

As usual, the cornea specialist had no explanation for the problem. The cornea was slowly clouding over, but he insisted that I would still be able to see out of it for a long time. He felt that my problem was a retina problem.

When I got to Dr. Trese's office, his staff greeted me warmly. One of the ladies gave me a great hug and asked excitedly, "How are you doing? It's your one-year anniversary!"

I burst into great hiccupping sobs.

"Oh, you don't have to say anything." She hugged me again, and I laid my head on her shoulder as if she were my mother. She led me back to an exam room.

Dr. Trese had no explanation for my loss of sight. My retina was in stable condition. He advised that I come back in a few weeks.

In February 2000, I returned for another exam. A small amount of vision had returned since December, but I knew that something was wrong. When I arrived at the cornea specialist's office, I confronted him. He finally spoke the words I did not want to hear. "That transplant has failed," he said matter-of-factly after examining the eye.

Failed. What did that mean? He didn't tell me, and he said he would not operate again unless it was necessary in order to enable Dr. Trese to see the retina. "It's too risky, and you won't get enough benefit out of it."

How could he imagine what benefit I might or might not get from another transplant? I was angry. I was the one who lived with the vision loss every day. I was the one who had cried uncontrollably in Dr. Trese's office because I could no longer see an object in my hand.

I had suspected that the transplant was failing for several months. Even though I did not know what failure meant, I knew that vision loss did not mean failure; and I had planned for this day. I asked for a referral to another specialist. Perhaps the new doctor would also refuse. If so, I would accept the fact that I had done what could be done.

Reluctantly, the doctor gave me the name of a cornea specialist in Indiana. I talked with Dr. Trese, and he agreed that a second opinion was worth obtaining. He could no longer see the retina clearly, but he felt that it remained stable.

I waited for several months before deciding to visit the new doctor. I tried to assess the seriousness of the problem, to know how much vision I had really lost. Just as I was about to make up my mind and make the appointment, my vision improved so much that I was unwilling to risk losing it to complications of another transplant.

The improvement was temporary. In December 2000, I caught the flu and another upper respiratory infection, and I again lost all of my vision. I called and made an appointment before I could change my mind.

The new doctor talked very openly about factors which might influence the success of another transplant, including matching the approximate age of the donor cornea and my body. He sent some pamphlets home for me to read, and another transplant was scheduled for March 13, 2001.

The second transplant was, overall, more successful than the first. My cornea remained clear for six months, and I did not experience vision loss at all during the first year.

In time, though, my vision did begin to blur; and the cornea began to cloud. The transplant was eventually pronounced another failure. The doctor advised against more attempts because of the high risk of rejection. He informed me of some research that was being done on artificial corneas, stating that he felt I would be a good candidate for one of the procedures, and discussed pros and cons of various types with me. I left disappointed, but I felt that I had been treated with respect and that the doctor was not simply refusing to provide treatment because he was uncertain of the potential benefits.

25

UNWANTED MAJORITY STATUS

Being in the majority generally has "perks" that make it a desirable status. That is, unless the majority you're in is the one in which I have spent most of my life: the 70 percent of blind people who are unemployed. Researchers are well aware of the impact that unemployment has on African Americans, women, men…almost any kind of person one can identify. Most people have the ability to overcome unemployment in a relatively short amount of time. It is common to hear a person talk about being unemployed for eight or nine months, which may seem like quite a long time. I have never heard of a nondisabled person who was unemployed for six or seven years—except stay-at-home moms. Prolonged unwanted unemployment truly does take a toll on a person, especially when there seems to be no way out of the situation.

In early 1999, I arranged to take two classes at Anderson University and transfer the credits to SFA in order to meet the final requirements for my graduation. I looked forward to finally finishing the degree and getting on with life. People kept telling me that there were many jobs that just required a four-year degree. Surely, I would be able to find one.

THE JOB SEARCH

I applied for several jobs during 1999 without success. Some were jobs which would require me to handle a lot of paperwork or input data from forms filled out in handwriting. One was, I perceived, an ideal position for me. I would be working as an educational assistant for a child with multiple disabilities. And as if I wasn't excited enough in the first place, the interview was scheduled on my birthday!

The school was located in another town, quite far from where I lived. My mom and I made a trip to town and drove home later that day. I spent the morning observing the child and his teachers and talking with the assistant who held the job at the time.

When I went into the interview with the principal in the afternoon, I felt confident that I had a good chance of being hired. The principal asked a lot of questions about how I would handle situations involving the child's disabilities and modifications that I might need because of blindness. None of these had a negative impact on me until she asked, "Will you be all right living so far away from your parents?"

Why would she ask such a question? Did it have to do with the fact that Mom was sitting out in the lobby waiting? I was mortified. Trying hard to stay calm, I informed her that I had attended college 1,100 miles away from home and had lived independently for several years. Looking back, I don't believe that I should have offered her an answer to the question except to ask whether she asked the same when interviewing other applicants who would need to relocate.

REJECTION

I was not offered the job. I was sent a form letter which provided no legitimate information about the reason for my rejection. The job was offered to the only other applicant: a sighted person with no experience or training in special education or any related area. My resume was not even submitted to the school board for consideration. When I provided it, the board confronted the principal, who stated that I would need to be led around the building and therefore hiring me would be inappropriate.

I was shocked. I had thoroughly discussed my plan for learning the layout of the school building during the interview. The school building would be open during the summer, and my plan had been to hire someone to spend a few days orienting me before I began work officially. The real concern, it seemed, was my inability to observe the child visually during his travels throughout the school and ensure that he didn't trip or become injured because he was blind. In addition to the loss of dignity I felt, I was saddened that the child was not afforded an education that would recognize a blind person's ability to travel independently despite the fact that he was learning the skills needed for safe and independent travel. Without using these skills, what good is the learning?

INCIDENT ON THE STAIRS

I attended the convention of the National Federation of the Blind in Atlanta, Georgia, that summer. The convention was held in a hotel with a large open area with an atrium in the middle. Travel between the first and second floor could be accomplished by taking the elevator, an escalator, or a flight of stairs. The hotel layout was confusing even for sighted people, including some of the employees. For a blind person—and especially a disoriented blind person—navigation was very difficult.

One afternoon, I began to feel the familiar "fuzzy brain"—similar to a partial seizure. Knowing that I needed to rest, I left the event I had been attending and began to make my way—I thought—to the escalator, intending to go downstairs and cross the street to my room in the overflow hotel.

I never found the escalator. I became disoriented and experienced lack of awareness of where I was. Unaware that my cane had detected a drop-off, I walked over the top of a flight of stairs and fell head-first, landing on my right hand and injuring nerves and muscles I used for working with a cane.

Several people stopped to ask if I was all right, and a man who I later learned was a national board member accompanied me to my hotel. Too tired to think about the embarrassment of falling on my face before a celebrity, I pulled back the covers and settled into bed for a very long nap. I knew at that moment that I needed a dog. A dog would have stopped at the top of that flight of stairs and not moved forward without my command. I would not have given that command without being aware of what I was doing.

DORI

In September 1999, I traveled back to Morristown, New Jersey, to train with a new dog. Getting my new dog marked a turning point in my life. I soon became more active in the childcare ministry and the choir at church—in fact, at the very church where I balked at meeting the greeter. I also began working as a freelance writer.

Dori, the new dog, was a spunky black Labrador retriever who loved children and could play for hours. She was a tremendous comfort to young children in the church nursery, where I worked part-time; and she was a faithful and serene presence onstage when I sang with the choir.

Dori was a good worker and bravely accompanied me to a writers' convention in Chicago; the American Council of the Blind convention in Des Moines, Iowa; various childcare settings; and numerous family gatherings. However, she was deeply affected by stress. Her stress-prone nature unfortunately resulted in the development of chronic infections and behaviors which were difficult to control. In the fall of 2001, I retired her after many months of expensive veterinary care, hard work, deliberation, and grief.

Retiring Dori was one of the most painful decisions I ever had to make. I was on the verge of making important decisions about graduate school. Training with a new dog meant putting those decisions on hold. I didn't know it at the time, but training with a new dog also opened up new opportunities that would change the course of my life.

MUTED

Sitting in the restaurant, I was impressed with the quietness of the music in the background. I enjoyed hearing the music; but it was also nice to eat in a place where there were not many competing conversations. I turned my head to the right to hear what my mom was saying—and we both stopped the conversation in shock.

"Did you just turn your head all the way to the right?" she asked.

"I guess I did." I couldn't deny that I had done it, and I was frightened about what it meant. I was having difficulty hearing.

An audiogram revealed that I had a very mild hearing loss. "It's really not very significant," the audiologist told me.

But it was significant to me, and it continued to increase over the next year. An instructor from the Seeing Eye loaned me a pair of reverse-slope hearing aids to use for a few months because I was having difficulty hearing some traffic sounds and conversing with people in certain environments. Eventually, I needed to return the aids, and several more years passed before I found a way to get some that were suited for my own needs. In time, I accomplished this by writing a proposal to the vocational rehabilitation agency and explaining that my hearing loss was deeply impactful to me as a blind person since I could not rely on sight as a way to compensate for it.

Adjusting to hearing loss was very difficult for me. When adapting to blindness, I could tell people that I needed more lighting or contrast, that an object was not big enough for me to see it, that I could not read print or identify a picture, etc. When explaining what I cannot hear, things were not so simple.

Because I heard sounds more clearly when they were behind

me, I preferred to walk ahead of people. Wherever I walked, conversation was inhibited while walking. In social situations,, I preferred to sit with my back to a wall so that conversations behind me didn't interfere with my participation in the conversation at my own table.

Since I experienced difficulty in locating the sources of sounds, I learned to request that people identify their location when I asked where they are instead of just saying, "Here." I also learned to ask them to repeat and speak more clearly instead of asking, "What?"

Because sounds are made up of several frequencies, recognizing a sound depends on hearing all of the frequencies consistently. My hearing loss was not the same across all frequencies; and it fluctuated from day to day. As it changed, I sometimes found myself unable to recognize a sound that was once familiar. I might be unable to hear or recognize one person's voice in a crowd, etc.

I was shocked to discover that I could hear a car from several blocks away while wearing hearing aids! The funding difficulties that I experienced are extremely common. Insurance will pay for glasses for a person whose sight is slightly impaired but who is still able to drive; but one must be severely hearing impaired before insurance will pay for hearing aids, even if one does not have the sight that is needed in order to compensate for hearing loss.

THE SEARCH CONTINUED

I continued applying for jobs. However, my search for full-time employment was unfruitful. Eventually, J.J. offered me a job working part-time in the nursery. I kept this job for two and a half years and eventually worked some additional hours in the church-operated day care. I loved the work but found the day care environment difficult to cope with because of poor acoustics. My hearing loss posed significant difficulties in environments where voices blended and echoed. I also experienced chronic respiratory infections and an increase in migraine frequency during 2000 and 2001.

STRIKING OUT ON MY OWN

The severity of my medical problems forced me to face important questions about my ability to hold down a full-time job. For a while, I worked from home so that I could allow myself to rest when I was ill or fatigued.

I was working in the earliest form of the gig economy. My experience was promising in that I found things that I could do. It was a dismal failure in terms of earning potential. In one instance, it shows how top-earning leaders take advantage of workers' passion and eagerness to earn in order to generate work. In another case, it shows that some types of work are very difficult for a person with a disability to do without help from others.

In May 2000, I applied for a position as a "Guide" with About, Inc. and was hired as an independent contractor to set up a web site providing information related to blindness. The position seemed promising. I could write as much as I wanted to write and, according to the company, the more I wrote, the more people would visit the web site and the more I would be paid.

In November 2000, the company paid for the writers to attend a conference at an expensive hotel. I wondered why they didn't take that money and pay us more. It never occurred to me that the pay would have been fairly limited. I just knew that it would be a lot more than I was currently earning.

At the conference, editors talked about how our passion for our topics should drive our work and we shouldn't worry about our earnings. I began to feel uncomfortable.

By April 2001, I was dissatisfied with my earnings, which rarely reached more than $500 per month. I quit the company, took down my content, and rewrote it for my own web site.

My parents bought a duplex, and I rented the upstairs apartment from them while surviving on Supplemental Security Income and the small amount of money I was earning from my work at the church and day care.

In September 2001, I decided to sign up as a representative with two direct sales companies selling books and toys for children. I liked the prospect of having parties where I could both meet people and demonstrate and sell products. My first two home parties were quite successful.

My efforts with direct sales presented two problems. I needed reliable transportation for myself and my inventory; and I would need money to pay for booths at fairs and other events where I could demonstrate and sell products. I soon discovered that while I enjoyed selling books and toys, this would not be a viable source of stable income for me.

In the fall of 2001, I went back to the Seeing Eye to train with my third dog, a tiny yellow Labrador retriever named Meghan.

Meghan loved our days working in the nursery. She was gentle, and children threw their arms around her and went to her for comfort when the environment was chaotic.

TECHNICAL WRITER

In the summer of 2002, a friend who had been in dog guide training with me gave me a job tip. An adaptive technology company was planning to hire someone as an independent contractor to handle some overflow technical writing assignments. I applied and was hired to write help topics for assistive hardware and software products for people who were blind.

I had become so accustomed to instability of income and part-time employment that I was surprised when a friend said to me, "You're now part of the 30 percent!" I began to pay off bills and purchase items that I had previously only dreamed about being able to afford.

I enjoyed my assignments and eventually moved to Florida to continue my work on site. Inca and Meghan went with me, and we all settled into a spare bedroom at my friend's house. Inca was accustomed to being the lone cat; and she became one of six cats in the house.

Working on site gave me a greater appreciation for the adaptive technology products I used every day. I was taking part in the creation of some incredibly complex masterpieces!

The move to Florida and the newfound income cost me my eligibility for Medicaid. I began to search for new means of treating my migraines and respiratory problems, unable to afford the

12 medications I had been taking. My search led me to information about the use of nutritional supplements, essential oils, and the South Beach Diet. My respiratory problems vanished for two years, but my migraines remained difficult to control.

My work came to an abrupt halt in February 2003, with no explanation. I experienced bouts of severe panic.

My roommate, who also worked at the company, encouraged me to calm myself by thinking practically. "What are we working on right now?" she asked. When I made a list, she said, "We will need you."

Days went by, and then weeks, then months without work. Other full-time employees said to me, "You'll need to have other irons in the fire." I wondered what irons they had in the fire since I was the only one who was working as a contractor.

Several months later, I learned that there would be no more work for me. The company was downsizing and had even laid off several salaried employees. I had been flung back into 70 percent. I began to look for any kind of work I could do with a degree in psychology.

JOB INTERVIEWS

I took a taxi out to an agency that advertised for a group home supervisor to work in the evenings. The interviewer began by telling me that the job required a driver's license because the person would need to transport residents.

"How many people are working during this time?" I asked.

"One. It would be you."

"Would it be permissible to take them using the bus?"

"No."

"Is there a possibility of hiring a driver as a reasonable accommodation?"

"We don't have the budget for that."

We sat in awkward silence for a few moments. Finally, I picked up my purse, struggling to push away my tears.

"Do you want to continue this interview?" he asked.

"Is there a possibility that you would hire me?" I asked, knowing what the answer would be.

I don't remember him saying, "No." I also don't remember the ride home.

My roommates and I had a preferred taxi driver who left his cell phone number with us and drove us on many of our trips to job interviews. On one such trip, one of my roommates and I rode 30 miles to fill out applications for childcare positions at a staffing agency. We were both running out of money, and the taxi trip would use up most of our remaining funds. But we supposed that since we both had previous childcare experience and the jobs only required high school diplomas, surely we had good chances of getting hired.

Oh, how silly of us! As soon as we walked into the door with our beautiful dog guides, the trouble began.

"Do you girls know that these are *childcare* jobs? cooed a lady in an extremely high-pitched voice, drawing out the words *childcare*.

"Yes, we do," I said, lowering my voice. "We both have experience, and we're here to apply."

We never got the applications filled out. On the way home, another passenger was riding in the front of the taxi. She cooed, "Are your dogs like your kids?"

As I tried to think of something polite to say that would not reveal my anger at being cooed at, our taxi driver saved the day. He said, "I think that's a different relationship." After a long pause, he said, "Their cats are their kids."

26

LEAVING CHURCH, RETURNING TO CHURCH

While I tried to find a church in Florida, I struggled deeply with memories of church and feelings about the ways that people interacted with me. I had some very positive memories of nurturing relationships with adults during my teen years. Working in the nursery had also been an extremely positive experience. But my deepest desire—and the desire which had most often gone unmet—had been to form friendships that would extend outside of church.

I was painfully aware of what I was missing. I heard people laughing with each other. I knew that they weren't laughing at me. I also knew that they were not laughing with me. Often a person said hello and then walked away without my knowledge. I was saddened when I heard the person talking to someone else across the room. The conversations never involved questions about how a person wrote in braille or how old their dog was. They were about how their kids were doing in school, what they did yesterday, what they thought of this or that candidate for office, and all kinds of other topics. I knew that she had found her preferred conversation partner, and I was not it.

The more emotionally wounded I became, the more I needed the healing community of believers in Christ. Yet the more I sought that community, the more I seemed to be wounded. What was the answer for the problem? When I ran out of emotional strength, how should I continue to face rejection from God's people?

While I was still working at the technology company, one of my roommates and I attended a small nondenominational church. We both joined the choir and went to some Bible study meetings with a young people's group.

I grew a bit hopeful about the general experience there when I began to develop a friendship with a couple who were near my age. But I realized how different our experiences were one afternoon when I was visiting their home.

"What are you doing about your retirement?" the young lady asked.

I listened to her three children playing in the pool. I leaned back on her overstuffed couch and took stock of her large home. Retirement? I was never going to retire! I had made a whopping $6,000 in fifteen years since my high school graduation! My income was $600 per month that came from the government! I wouldn't have a retirement!

We drifted apart over the weeks that followed. I wondered who I was kidding, trying to relate to all the working people at church. I had nothing to talk about with them.

I bounced from church to church, accepting rides from

gracious elderly people but never forming friendships. Meanwhile, my depression related to unemployment and other aspects of my life grew deeper.

During the spring of 2004, I attended a church with a large singles group that held meetings on Wednesday nights. Most of the attendees were young professionals in their late 20s and early 30s. I hoped that I would learn to fit into this group since I was just past 30 and was working at a technology company as a technical writer.

One evening, the group met to watch *The Passion* and discuss its impact. I brought a notepad and a slate and stylus, a manual tool that I used to write notes in braille. Before everyone settled down, I made a few notes to myself about some thoughts I was having.

While I was writing, someone leaned in very close to me. "Oh, is that how you write?" she asked, drawing out her words as if speaking to a child. "What did you write?"

I had no desire to read what I had written aloud. It was private. But there was no polite way to say this to her. I answered, "It is a personal reminder to myself," and felt quite rude for not displaying the fact that I knew how to read.

On the next Sunday morning, someone picked me up and we arrived early enough to overhear some conversation between other members of the Bible study class. "Are you still driving the crazies around?" asked one man.

"Yeah, that's my job, driving for the mental health center," said another.

I decided then that this would be my last time attending there.

If I received therapy for my depression and needed transportation, I would be one of his "crazies." Was it too much of me to expect that Christians might hold better attitudes about people who had mental illness?

I did not return to church for several months. I was certain that it was not possible for me to find a home in any church. My roommate tried another church and felt very comfortable. She continued to invite me each week to go with her. "The people are really nice," she said.

Finally, I agreed to go, just once. If I didn't like it, I wouldn't go back.

My experiences with mystical spirituality are not things to trust my entire life's growth on. But once in a while God uses them to pull me out of a deep, dark place. Once, during my undergraduate years at AU, a friend sent me a letter on a cassette tape. Our letters were always a mixture of monologues about important topics and restless chatter with music in the background. At one point, she was turning the radio dial and heard a beautiful song; but the radio station was extremely faint. The song faded in and out and many of the words could not be heard.

On that Sunday morning, thirteen years later, someone sang that beautiful song. The words from Psalm 51 pricked at a deep place in my heart, confronting my attitudes about myself and things I had done in my selfish desire to be happy. As I heard the words and let them flow into my soul, I knew that I was at the right church. But there still remained the problem of my woundedness related to lack of friendships at church.

I tried discussing my relational difficulties with a pastor when

I was fairly young. His answer stung deeply, and it stayed with me for many years. "You have two choices," he said gruffly. "You can either be a hermit and stay home, or you can come anyway."

I continued to attend church—I enjoyed the teaching and the music. But I felt that perhaps God did not want me to have fellowship with other people. Perhaps I had done something bad. Perhaps aloneness was a punishment. Perhaps God was angry with me for not spending enough time with Him, and so He caused me to experience repeated rejection, removing the possibility that I might spend time with anyone else.

I was aware on some level that this thinking was flawed, I had a difficult time correcting it. Thinking differently required an extreme measure of faith that I could not call forth.

I needed to do something different at the new church. I requested a meeting with the pastor, where I told him about my struggle and my desire for friendships in the church.

His response was very brief, but it spoke volumes. "You reach out, and I will pray."

What a simple but powerful thing! Of course, he could not fix the problem. But he believed in the power of prayer, and he recognized that I couldn't break down this barrier by myself; so, he did what he was capable of doing.

I did make a friend in that church. In fact, she became an accountability partner during the few months of my remaining time in Florida. Although my time at the church was brief, I learned that sometimes the body of Christ does not fail—and I really am a part of it.

My friendship with Amy led to an invitation for me to

participate on the worship team. I accepted and began writing songs after a lengthy period of inactivity. I also participated in a weekly Bible study group until I moved back to Indiana. This intensive study opened my heart and mind to things I needed to think about in the years to come.

27

INDEPENDENCE VS. AUTONOMY

My time in Florida gave me several opportunities to think about two important words that I had been using interchangeably: independence and autonomy. I learned while I was in Florida that while I might not be able to do something independently, I might still be able to do it autonomously. That is, I might still make my own choices and direct the outcome of the situation. This new understanding set in motion important changes in my thinking and, ultimately, in the way that I lived my life.

Transportation difficulties can be one of the greatest sources of frustration for people with visual impairments or other disabilities where driving is limited or not possible. Often this difficulty masquerades as grief over loss of driving ability. Driving is the familiar solution to the deeper loss: the loss of control over where, when, and how quickly one travels. Driving is a symbol of adulthood in our independent society; yet given an equally effective means of controlling one's coming and going, the loss of physical ability might not be so emotionally devastating.

Sometimes people mistake the ability to drive for independence. I am aware that many people who are blind enjoy having the experience of driving a car in an open area so that they can feel the sensation of driving. For me, this experience has never been alluring. I expressed my feelings once in a journal following an encounter with a stranger:

The cab driver who took me to school one morning asked if I ever wanted to drive. I said yes because I do. I'd love to be able to drive, just for the simple reason that I could take myself places and if I was late, it would be my own fault. He asked if I had ever gotten to drive in a parking lot. I know that in movies that is a big deal, and I wish I could say how mad it makes me. Do people really think that driving in a parking lot is a big thrill? It's fake, and driving is something I could care less about. I don't want to just play at some driving game. Driving is about independence, and for me to drive in some parking lot is a mockery of my need for independence. It would be ok for me to play at independence, but it doesn't matter to people that I can never meet real needs I have.

When I lived in Florida, I often rode the bus to the shopping center, went to my store of choice, and requested assistance from a customer service representative. When I was finished, I called a cab or took the bus home. A sighted person could have completed the errand in a bit less time, but I was in relatively good control of my own coming and going as long as I allowed a bit of extra time to wait for my transportation. When I was working, I had enough extra money that I could choose to take a cab to a restaurant to eat or to pick up some fast food. These things allowed me to live a comparable life to the one I suppose I would lead if I was sighted. The inability to drive was not an issue unless I needed or wanted to go somewhere where the bus did not go, or unless the cab cost was prohibitive.

When my neurological symptoms became difficult to control, I experienced difficulty traveling due to disorientation and seizure-like episodes. I was also experiencing difficulty due to changes in my hearing. An orientation and mobility instructor assisted me in developing strategies to cope with the impact of my various disabilities on my ability to travel independently. We worked to determine whether I could safely cross streets, how to determine when I might need to use paratransit instead of the bus, and some possible strategies for coping with disorientation episodes. I began to realize that I did not need to become a person who could do all things, that it was all right for me to seek assistance or take a cab when another person would have taken the bus. I began to accept that the goal, getting where I wanted to go, was what mattered. How I did it really did not matter very much.

RETURNING HOME

Unemployment was a frustrating experience for me in Florida that would probably have continued for quite a long time if one thing had not happened. In the fall of 2004, four hurricanes hit Florida one after the other in August and September.

I began to think about the meaning of the words "independence" and "autonomy" in a different light.

Going through so many major storms in a month caused me to take a long look at my need for assistance from people in the community. In a disaster situation people very often are in the midst of caring for their own families and aren't able to assist no matter how much they want to.

I've always taken living independently for granted—I can do my own cooking, cleaning, etc. The most important aspect of living on my own is preparedness for the unknown. The average preparedness advice includes putting up storm shutters and having a first-aid kit, food and water ready. For a person with disabilities, preparedness also includes the ability to get oneself to safety. I had to admit that I didn't have the resources to live independently in Florida. If I had a job and could establish a large emergency fund, I could get myself out. But I didn't and couldn't.

Evacuation procedures caused me a lot of stress. I didn't have the luxury of choosing to drive away somewhere, which is what I would do if I could see. The only evacuation mechanism available to me was flying. I couldn't fly myself in and out over and over, let alone my animals. I took a lot of risks and chose to stay in town during the first two storms. Hurricane preparedness took a major toll on my emotional health.

I boarded my cats during the first hurricane. The experience was quite traumatic for them. I stayed with my friend from church. When the storm had passed, she confided in me that if it had been a direct hit her family would not have been adequately prepared and she felt that I should take better precautions for myself.

The second storm primarily impacted the eastern part of the state. My roommates and I did not evacuate. We had no place to go.

One of my roommates, Amy, and I stood on the porch during the early hours of the storm, listening to the wind and rain. We were not aware enough at the time to realize how dangerous this was. We were fortunate at the time that the ground was not soaked yet.

The third storm was a category 4 storm which came up the western coast. By this time, the writing was on the wall for me. I packed up most of my belongings and flew to Indiana with my cats and Meghan.

I couldn't move all at once. I shipped as much as I could ahead of time and flew home with as many packed bags as I could. I returned later to finish moving.

When I returned, a surprise awaited me. Our tree had fallen and blocked the front door—right in a place where Amy and I had stood as the tropical storm-force winds of hurricane Frances blew. By the time I arrived, the tree had been chopped and stacked at the end of our front sidewalk. As I stood at our door, I could see it all the way at the end of the walk.

Seeing the tree humbled me and impressed upon me what the storms could do. I didn't want to go home, where I felt that no jobs or friends awaited me. But I realized why it was the best option for me.

When I got home to Indiana, there were signs that all would be well. My parents had never rented out my apartment. My furniture was all in the same old places. Inca tore out of her carrier, found her old favorite chair, and settled down for a great purry nap. Sable and Sierra, the two cats I acquired in Florida, took a little longer to settle down. But eventually they, too, made my upstairs apartment their home.

During the last two months of my time in Florida, I began to experience severe vertigo associated with migraine. It didn't go away when I moved back to Indiana. For many months, I sat down to go up and down stairs to my apartment; slowed down greatly when walking through open space and spent a lot more time cutting vegetables at my dining room table instead of while standing at my kitchen counter.

I had always been proud of my ability to do things for myself. This pride developed as a sort of consequence to achieving goals that were part of the learning processes of my childhood and adolescence. Everything I learned was a stepping-stone on the path toward independent life. Therefore, independent life was something that must happen and must be maintained.

As I began to come to terms with the disabilities I acquired later, I rebuilt my understanding of how to live my life. While I was grateful to be able to do things for myself because it gave me more freedom to choose the time and place to do them, it didn't really matter if I had help in doing something and still accomplished the same goal. It didn't matter whether I drove or walked myself or hired someone to drive for me. What mattered was that I got to my destination.

28

THE ALPHACOR

In May of 2004, I learned that the artificial cornea recommended by my former cornea specialist had been approved for use in the United States and was available in Jacksonville, Florida. Because the evaluation and device were not covered by Medicaid, I began working hard to raise money. In July, I traveled to Jacksonville for the evaluation and learned that I was a candidate for the procedure.

After returning home to St. Petersburg, I began brainstorming about ways to raise several thousand dollars to cover the cost of the surgery and the cornea. My plans were interrupted by my move back to Indiana.

I experienced feelings of disappointment following the move. The doctor in Jacksonville had been so positive! I wondered if doctors closer to home were doing the procedure.

I did a Google search using the keywords Alphacor and Indianapolis. I was pleasantly surprised when my results included the web site of the Price Vision Group. I called and made an appointment for another evaluation.

The doctor who evaluated me in Indianapolis requested that I travel to Detroit for an examination with Dr. Trese to be certain that the condition of my retina was stable before work on my cornea was performed. The result of the exam in Detroit was encouraging, and surgery was scheduled for February 15, 2005.

"WHAT WILL SHE SEE?"

Before my surgery, Alphacor implants had been covered with a flap of skin from the white part of the eye. I was awake during the procedure and experienced pain several times that required more anesthetic medication. At the first time, I began to shake uncontrollably. I was aware of discomfort in the eye and could feel the movement of something against it. However, I could not move or speak.

"Can you feel that?" the doctor asked in alarm. "Give her more pain block."

I began to drift, but it happened again. My eyes began to tear.

"It's happening again," the doctor said. "More pain block please."

As I began to drift, I heard one of the techs from the company say, "I wonder what she'll be able to see tomorrow."

"I'm not supposed to be able to see for three months," I protested in my mind. But I could say nothing.

I found out the following day that a piece of my old cornea had been used instead of the flap of white skin. As long as the piece of cornea remained clear, removing it would not be necessary—and I would be able to see.

DISCOVERIES AND LIMITS

My visual ability did not improve over time as it had when my retina was reattached. However, as I became more active in the weeks following surgery and ventured into new environments, I discovered more things that I could see. Some were things that weren't found in my home. Others were things that appeared differently in lighting outside my home.

The artificial cornea had limitations that I did not learn about until much later. In time, I began to experience the gray curtain again. I developed a scar tissue membrane behind the cornea that was hindering my vision. Surgery in 2007 provided some relief; but this was limited. In the spring of 2008, the membrane returned, and the specialist felt there was no more that could be done.

I descended into a great depression. I had the skills to live with blindness, but the emotional impact of being told there was no hope was very great.

By this time, I had begun attending Park Place Church of God in Anderson, Indiana, and was attending seminary at Anderson University. On the Wednesday evening following my exam with the cornea specialist, I was seated in the choir beside Leta, a long-time friend of the family.

As I requested prayer from the choir and explained what the doctor had said to me, Leta took my hand. When I was finished speaking, we sang another song. Leta just held my hand as we sang. The choir prayed for me at the end of rehearsal—a prayer that was a balm for my weary soul. But I knew that Leta was already praying as we sang.

Sometimes there are no answers to the questions I ask about why something happens. But the presence of a community who knows they don't need to try to answer the questions, who knows it is enough to simply be with me in the midst of the pain, is a healing balm to the soul.

SCARY ROLLER COASTERS

For several years, I did nothing more about my eye. Since nothing could be done, I did not go to any eye doctors. I had plenty of other things to manage. I was seeing a specialist to manage asthma, one to manage migraines, and one to manage rheumatoid arthritis that had been diagnosed in 2007. I got used to life as it was.

In 2011, an error in interpretation of an MRI led a doctor to tell me that my eyes were deteriorating. This provoked a visit to Dr. Trese. I traveled without any hope. In fact, I was prepared for him to speak to me about the possibility of removing my eyes. Perhaps this would make it possible for me to experience less pain.

The exam went much differently from what I expected. The pressure in my eyes was healthy, and I still had the ability to see some color contrast and movement. These things indicated that I might benefit from new techniques that Dr. Trese had been using to treat scar tissue membranes.

I returned home with surgery scheduled for September of 2011. When I shared my good news with the choir, Leta was sitting beside me again. The same community that grieved with me when I was told that nothing more could be done rejoiced with guarded hope as I waited for another surgery.

The procedure was successful in restoring some sight. The church community bore witness to my adjustment to the restoration of a small amount of sight. They asked questions about what I was able to see and how they could change the ways they were giving information to me.

Dr. Trese continued to provide care as the membrane grew back every few years until 2020. I kept track of my eye health and the progress of my other medical conditions meticulously. I noticed that each time I lost sight suddenly, I had recently had a flare-up of my autoimmune condition. Dr. Trese didn't see typical signs of autoimmune damage, but I continued to keep track of the progress of the two conditions.

Dr. Trese performed his last procedure with me in 2020. The procedure was extremely painful. I am allergic to several medications used for pain control following surgery. I often sleep a lot following surgery in order to give my eye an opportunity to heal gently. In 2020, I was in the midst of academic study and returned to class quickly.

I met with my classes on Zoom since COVID was still going around and I wanted to protect my health. My professors gave me permission to keep my camera off during class meetings. I rested on my couch while listening to class discussions and followed along with class notes on my wireless braille display.

In 2022, I attempted to have another procedure to treat the membrane. Dr. Trese was not in the office at the time, and I was given no information about when he would return. So, I had the procedure done by another doctor.

My eye did not tolerate the procedure. Before I knew the

results, I felt them in my heart. I woke from surgery with music in my head, reminding me that whatever happened, God was faithful. I knew that I would carry on, held in that faithfulness, with praise in my heart and my mouth.

I did not attend church gatherings from 2020 through late 2022. How I missed having someone hold my hand after I said the words, "There is nothing left to do." The music that I heard in my mind comforted me.

Dr. Trese did not return. He died in the fall of 2022. I was deeply grieved at the loss of my beloved doctor who had played such an important role in my life for so long. My grief was shared around the world by thousands of families. Most of his care was provided to very small premature infants.

Since that time, I have guarded my autoimmune health very closely. Without knowing whether this contributes to the growth of the membrane, I assume that caring for this aspect of my health will be beneficial in all ways.

I still have very limited sight which is still somewhat useful. One day I must live without it. Today I am grateful for it and choose to treat it as a gift and to use it for whatever time it remains.

29

GETTING PAST THE GRAY CURTAIN

After my discussion with college dormmates in 1991, I struggled to comfort myself with the thought that God allowed me to be blind so that I could manifest His glory. It was a difficult thing to conceptualize at the time. As I grew older and lived more of my life, I began to see how this was happening. Because I knew what it was like to experience aloneness, I was able to understand other people's feelings of aloneness. Because I knew what it was to struggle with God, I understood other people's spiritual struggles and did not hurry them through the process of spiritual formation. Because I knew what it was to need God's comfort, I encouraged others as they pursued Him with passion and hunger. Because I could not simply look at someone and assume I understood their response while speaking to a group, I called response forth, developing community instead of allowing people to exist in isolated togetherness. Healing would have provided me a nice benefit; but it might have robbed the community of benefit that they needed.

This didn't mean that I stopped wanting healing or praying for it. As the gray curtain has returned every so often, so have all the feelings that come with it. As I experience great physical pain in my eyes, I ask God to please take it away without making me have to go through removal of the eye. I would not be human if I didn't do these things.

Dr. Trese was used to working with people who will one day lose their sight, and his goal was to help his patients maintain use of their sight for as long as possible. When I reported severe pain and asked if he could just remove the eye, he took ultrasound scans and encouraged me to reconsider while treatment options were still available.

My prayers are sometimes cries of the soul that God understands better than I can express. When I ask God to take away pain, God knows better than I how to give what I need. As I lose sight in my eye and approach the time of the gray curtain, light itself often becomes painful. Treatment of the eye relieves pain. Dr. Trese's words were wise. Now that the eye cannot tolerate surgery well, more wisdom will be required in the future.

God made me and God can use me in whatever state I am in. This is absolutely true, and it is the truth that I remember when things are hard.

I know how to live without sight. I have skills to use my other senses and all kinds of talking apps, braille on my appliances, etc. I miss the things I was once able to see. But they are not central to my experience of joy.

I feel a deep sense that comes forth when I remember the words, "There is nothing left to do," and when I read the articles about long-term complications of the artificial cornea procedures. These articles tell a story that isn't part of what news articles say to the public. Many people who receive artificial corneas experience rejection and painful complications, including total blindness and need for removal of the eye.

I signed a lot of papers with hard legal words written on them. I knew the words—they were all read to me. I understood that there was no guarantee of success. I understood that I would need to comply with all the doctor's instructions and that I would need to take anti-rejection medication for the rest of my life. I was willing to do these things. In fact, when I sought out the new doctor I wrote out a detailed explanation stating that I was interested in maintaining my eye health as much as possible after rejection of the artificial cornea. I expected no miracles. But without a doctor who is willing to treat me as a person with extremely little sight—or none at all—there is no way to maintain the health of my eye. There is no way to manage pain that may come from the implant.

When I realize that the doctors who provide experimental treatments often don't provide ongoing care to people who don't regain sight, a primal sense of anger and abandonment feeling rises up in me. I want to cry out, "Aren't I still worth anything?" "Why did you abandon me?"

I don't need more prayers for healing. I need to know, to trust, and experience that God does not abandon me. During 2022, as I struggled with the depth of emotions when my eye did not tolerate the last procedure, I was still isolating at home due to the prevalence of COVID. The physical isolation amplified the feelings of spiritual abandonment that I experienced. By this time, I was a member of the clergy, but I was also human and vulnerable to the need for feelings of closeness in my relationship with God.

I began attending church in person again in the fall of 2022; but I found that my needs were different from the needs I heard expressed around me. While other people were tired and wanted to rest, I was acutely aware of the remaining feelings of isolation and abandonment that could rise up within me at any moment. I needed to be connected with God and with community—with the community that was often too tired to connect.

Today, several years after waking from that unsuccessful surgery, I continue to cling to what remains.

God is faithful and strong. God will never leave or forsake me. God's Spirit abides with me. Forever.

www.ingramcontent.com/pod-product-compliance
Lightning Source LLC
Chambersburg PA
CBHW021707120626
46545CB00004B/1448